Other Books by Rokelle Lerner

Affirmations for Adult Children of Alcoholics

Affirmations for the Inner Child

Living in the Comfort Zone:
The Gift of Boundaries in Relationships

Building Relationships That Work

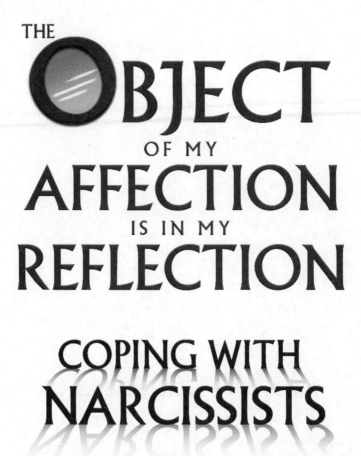

THE OBJECT OF MY AFFECTION IS IN MY REFLECTION

COPING WITH NARCISSISTS

ROKELLE LERNER

Health Communications, Inc.
Deerfield Beach, Florida

www.hcibooks.com

Library of Congress Cataloging-in-Publication Data

Lerner, Rokelle.
  The object of my affection is in my reflection / Rokelle Lerner.
    p. cm.
  Includes index.
  ISBN-13: 978-0-7573-0768-3 (trade paper)
  ISBN-10: 0-7573-0768-X (trade paper)
1. Narcissism.   I. Title.

  BF575.N35L47 2009
  158.2—dc22

                                                          2008033964

Publisher: Health Communications, Inc.
            3201 S.W. 15th Street
            Deerfield Beach, FL 33442-8190

Cover design by Andrea Perrine Brower
Inside formatting by Lawna Patterson Oldfield

In loving memory of my father,
Dr. Raphael Weisberg

Contents

Acknowledgments

*M*y heartfelt thanks to the following people: Mary Stangler for her patience and support; Jason Aeric Huenecke for his encouragement and insightful perspective; Mary McGuckian for her generosity, friendship, and sense of humor; Patricia Broat for her faith in me and her ability to motivate others; Gary Seidler, the coach; Cottonwood de Tucson, who allows me to continue to create and do the work I love to do; Lois Weisberg for her unwavering encouragement and her fantastic job as a proofreader; Sam Vaknin and Sandy Hotchkiss, whose work is an inspiration; Bonnie Burg for her expertise and guidance; Linda Bylander for her generosity of spirit and support; and to the men and women who have allowed me to witness their struggles and be a part of their healing.

Introduction

*T*his book is based on the premise that good relationships are the foundation of emotional health. Professional success, loving children, and loyal friends can't make up for the loneliness and pain of a primary relationship gone wrong. When that relationship is with a narcissist, your emotional health becomes so eroded that your sanity and your dignity disappear. No matter how hard you try, there is no way to apply a tourniquet to the perpetual drama and agony of living with an individual who is as wounded as the narcissist. The pain you experience living with a narcissistic partner bleeds into every aspect of life and robs you of your equanimity and your soul. My goal is to help people whose lives are impacted by this disorder and assist those professionals who treat these men and women.

Narcissism is most often defined as excessive self-love and grandiosity, but in fact, narcissism is better viewed as a continuum of emotional states from adolescent self-interest to romantic love to excessive self-absorption and entitlement. For example, when we fall in love we often worship or idealize our beloved and experience that idealization in return. Romantic love (which has been called temporary insanity) is a narcissistic state where we can become focused on our relationship and ourselves to the exclusion of everything and everyone. In addition, adolescents experience a predictable stage of narcissistic development that passes with time and maturity; or so we're told. However, pathological narcissism develops from early childhood wounds that manifest in a hunger for perfect attention and admiration that can never be satisfied. For the narcissist, these childhood deficits create a distorted worldview that they are entitled to adoration simply because they exist.

One of the challenges in describing narcissism is that it is often associated with the sense of self-entitlement that has become such a part of our culture that makes it difficult to discern narcissistic tendencies from pathological narcissism. The messages we receive from society, the emotional failure between parents and children, and the history of failed relationships that have become the norm, all contribute to this phenomenon. Sadly, we have a population of five-year-olds acting like they are forty, and forty-year-olds with the emotional maturity of five years old. From drama queens to bullies, our culture permeates with self-indulgence and a "you owe me" attitude that cuts across all socio-economic barriers and exists in all walks of life.

Throughout my career I've worked with many partners of narcissists who wind up feeling crazy and desperate—and with good reason! It's baffling when the person you fell in love with, who used to treat you so lovingly and thoughtfully, suddenly acts like you are an annoyance—or worse, the enemy. It's painful to watch this person in public, treating people with respect and generosity and doing nice things such as acknowledging their birthdays—while consistently ignoring you. Your friends may think he's quite a catch; people may adore him. And you may begin to feel as if there's something desperately wrong with you.

This scenario could also describe the narcissistic parent who is held up as a model by friends and acquaintances who tell you what a lucky child you are! In the privacy of the home, however, the narcissistic parent becomes uninterested, rude, critical, and demeaning. He or she picks at your faults, and there's nothing you can do to win favor. Through this book, I hope to provide some comfort to those who have lived in this unending cycle of idealization to rejection, adoration to hatred, and respect to disregard.

The purpose of this book is not to vilify narcissists. My purpose is to shed light on the destructive dynamics that occur in relationships with narcissists. We must have compassion for the wounded narcissists who suffer incomprehensible agony. The survival mechanisms narcissists develop were created as a defense for repeated emotional injuries. These defenses allowed them to endure the pain of a childhood filled with abandonment and shame. Narcissists are not inherently evil. Unfortunately their wounds compel them to act in ways that are unconscionable, damaging, and ultimately tragic. Beneath their façade of grandiosity, narcissists are anguished, tortured, and angry people. The purpose of this book is not to judge the morality of narcissists, but to help you cope with them in your life.

It's important to keep in mind that narcissists desperately long to be involved in a relationship but have expectations that inevitably cause misery and disillusionment in themselves and in their partners. Their wounds prevent them from experiencing human intimacy because their primary attachment is not to a person but to the procurement of adoration and attention. This doesn't make them bad; it makes them tragic and emotionally unavailable in relationships. And since narcissists often choose mates with narcissistic wounds, it's imperative that we focus on ourselves *first*, and resist the urge to diagnose our friends, lovers, or coworkers.

Several years into my practice, I began to see a disturbing pattern in many of my clients, particularly among recovering alcoholics and addicts. Well into their sobriety, these people continued to display grandiosity, entitlement, anger, and extreme sensitivity to the slightest suggestion of inattention. The interesting thing was that these men and women also could be disarming, gregarious, and charismatic. Then they would morph into a screaming or pouting child, complaining, for example, that I hadn't come out to greet them while they were in the waiting room (even if they arrived early and I was still with a client). I came to discover that underneath these tirades was a chasm of shame and excruciating anguish.

Realizing that narcissism is diagnosed in approximately 1 percent of the population, I began to ask myself a rather narcissistic question: *Have all of them decided to come to me?* After conferring with colleagues, we all acknowledged that the plethora of clients displaying entitlement, contempt, and hypersensitivity was increasing in everyone's practice. One therapist put it succinctly: "I've got so many clients with narcissistic styles, I wonder if it's coming from the water supply." As glib as this comment may sound, the effects of narcissistic wounds are rampant and reverberate with everyone who lives or works with narcissists. What became clear to me was that this area needed to be addressed for the sake of those in relationships with narcissists, as well as for the men and women that suffer from this disorder.

Narcissists create a web of seduction, intimidation, and control. Partners of narcissists often describe to me the feeling of being under a spell, trapped in their inability to leave and their reluctance to stay. But unlike the fairy tales and myths of old, there is no one who can rescue them from this spell. My hope is that spouses, partners, coworkers, and children of narcissists will use this book as a guide to help them emerge from the deep sleep of living or working with a narcissist—and regain their lives, their purpose, and their spirits.

PART

1

THE ROOTS OF
NARCISSISM

Entitlement, Rage, and Contempt: The Plight of Narcissists and Their Victims

*W*hen you're in relationship with a narcissist, you relinquish your identity and your soul to them. Their seduction is similar to a razor-sharp stiletto being waved in your face: it's so mesmerizing, you won't know you're bleeding to death until it's too late. But it's not your blood that a narcissist wants—it's your emotional energy and your individuality.

A true narcissist has no qualms about taking your money, your love, your admiration, your body, or your soul to satisfy their unquenchable hunger. And just as vampires cringe when they're in the presence of crosses or holy water, narcissists recoil at ordinary adult experiences such as boredom, uncertainty, accountability, and, most of all, having to give as well as receive. (Bernstein, 2002)

Narcissists use whatever institution is available to achieve their goal of draining your emotional energy and individuality—the office of the church, parental authority, a political party, or even a Little League team. Seduction is so easy when you're in command. They use whatever tool is at their disposal to captivate you, own you, and then devour you. And, when you're under their spell, you obey without question and gradually begin to join the procession of the living dead.

Until you really get to know narcissists, you may think that they're some of the most charming, compelling people you've ever met. They're fun to be around at parties, are engaging conversationalists, tell amusing stories, and give their opinion on everything in the world. They are charming, that is, until you get to know them; that's when you're at risk of becoming one of their victims. They need you, and they crave what you can give them. They're spoiled and wounded children, desperately in need of someone to be in awe of them.

The aim of narcissists is to possess you. You are required to be their unquestioning worshiper and to never criticize or disagree with them. If they do something wrong, you must approve; if they detest someone, you must detest them as well. Your identity ceases to exist and you become a mere reflection of their image. You become a clone with no clue about what you're really thinking or feeling because you are under their spell. If you become involved with a narcissist—because you are related to them or you are a friend, a business partner, or a lover—you will suffer. And it will likely take years before you know why. (McDonnell, 2007)

Narcissists are actors playing a part. They are expert liars and, even worse, they believe their own lies. Practiced in dishonesty, they can't tell the difference between their own version of the truth and a falsehood. Narcissists lie to themselves first, and then systematically and often deliberately torture others with their lies. They may take the past and re-arrange it to make themselves look good. They rarely, if ever, admit fault and they never say they're sorry.

The narcissist has been depicted in art, drama, and literature for centuries. When we look closely at our own culture, we see that many of our fairy tales, novels, and films are replete with stories that revolve around narcissistic men and women. The term "narcissism" is derived from the ancient Roman poet Ovid's myth of Narcissus and Echo. This story provides us with a better understanding of the inner torment of narcissists and the inevitable suffering of those who attempt to have relationships with them.

THE MYTH OF NARCISSUS AND ECHO

Zeus, the king of the Olympians, was known for his many love affairs. The young and beautiful nymph Echo would distract his wife, Hera, with long and entertaining stories while Zeus took advantage of the moment to pleasure himself with other water nymphs. When Hera discovered this trickery she punished Echo by taking away her voice—except to repeat ("echo") another's words.

Narcissus was a handsome young man who was greatly desired by the water nymphs. Echo was completely enamored of Narcissus and professed her love for him. He cruelly rejected her and, in her shame and grief, she faded away until all that remained was her echoing voice, still declaring her love. The nymphs were very angry and desired revenge. They petitioned the gods, who arranged for Narcissus to fall in love with his own reflection in a pond. Narcissus did indeed fall in love with his image and kept trying to embrace it, only to have it disappear every time. He was unable to leave his reflection, even though he received no response from it. He pined away and died, leaving a flower in his place.

This myth describes the tragic outcome of trying to entice a narcissist to pay attention to you, to be close to you, and to treat you with respect. But Echo had lost her voice and could only repeat what Narcissus was saying to her. Like so many men and women in narcissistic relationships, she lost her spirit, disowned her needs, and surrendered her life in pursuit of this beautiful young man.

It's difficult for those in relationships with narcissists to remember that these men and women are utterly obsessed with their own reflections. And just as Narcissus would not reach into the water to take a drink because he would have shattered his own image into thousands of pieces, true narcissists cannot afford the luxury of showing their humanness or exposing their needs.

Being human plagues narcissists. To show vulnerability shatters their image and leaves them with a raw shame that's so intolerable they often react with the rage of a wounded animal. They know that people love them, but in the end it means nothing. As one narcissistic addict wrote after studying this myth: "I hear echoes outside of me from those who love and care for me. But I don't *hear* their love; only echoes of what I want, what I need, and what I can never have."

There are many interpretations of Ovid's myth, but one that particularly makes sense to me is a Jungian explanation. Analysts say that Narcissus's fall was one of necessity. Although he spent his days pining over his reflection, it wasn't until he actually "fell into himself" and drowned that he could be at peace.

Here's a more modern-day fable.

Desperate Housewives is one of the most popular dramas on television. One character in the show is Bree, a young woman who turns entitlement into an art form. She is a gorgeous and cunning woman living in a suburban gossip mill, and she revels in her beauty and sexual exploits. In order to get what she wants, she lies, steals, and even murders with very little conscience. In elegant, expensive clothing, she is the consummate homemaker and bares her soul to anyone who will listen. She obsesses about her mangled love life. When asked the question, "Why are your problems so much bigger than everyone else's?" she answers, "Because they're mine!" We all know people like this; in fact, our culture is so narcissistic that it would seem that Narcissus or Bree is the boy or girl next door.

Another example of modern-day narcissism is reality television, which millions of Americans watch religiously. We can sit in the comfort of our living rooms and watch, as people do, everything from the banal to the obscene. Clearly this is a "Big Brother" society, defined not by George Orwell's vision in his novel *Nineteen Eighty-Four,* but by a contemporary television program showcasing voyeurism, self-indulgence, and egotism.

Even though Narcissus and Bree are fictional characters, both have qualities that can be used to describe destructive narcissists:

- Indifference to the needs or concerns of others.
- Strongly self-focused and self-absorbed.
- Lacking remorse.
- Emotionally shallow.
- Cannot relate to others in a meaningful way.
- Have overpowering needs for admiration and attention.
- Viewing themselves as unique and special.
- Are grandiose, arrogant, haughty, and contemptuous.
- Belief that they can only be understood by other special or high-status people or institutions.
- Extreme jealousy of others or belief that others are jealous of them.

Pathological narcissism is described in the *Diagnostic and Statistical Manual of Mental Disorders, Fourth Edition* (DSM-IV) as "narcissistic personality disorder." It's defined as "A pervasive pattern of grandiosity (in fantasy or behavior), need for admiration, and lack of empathy that begins by early adulthood and presents in a variety of contexts."

Although this definition is helpful in some ways, it is incomplete. Grandiosity, the need for admiration, and lack of empathy could describe many people, from the annoying teenager next door to the political despot committing atrocities. Since the term *narcissism* is used so frequently, it's important to examine the difference between a narcissistic personality disorder and a personality with narcissistic traits. Although an individual with the traits of a narcissist can be extremely distressing, their prognosis is much more optimistic. Pathological narcissism is much more destructive and insidious. Without this differentiation, we are in danger of underestimating the relational damage and pain that occur in the wake of the men and women who have this disorder.

*N*arcissism Versus Narcissistic Traits

*E*veryone possesses some narcissistic traits. Fortunately, qualities such as modesty, prudence, realism, and consideration for others prevent many people from regarding themselves as superior beings. (Baumeister & Vohs, 2007)

There's a big difference between a narcissistic personality style and a diagnosis of narcissistic personality disorder (NPD). The American Psychiatric Association estimates that only one in one hundred people meet the criteria for NPD. But thousands of individuals exhibit narcissistic traits and cause severe distress and pain in others. Sadly, many of these men and women never come to the attention of healthcare professionals because they don't recognize their own narcissism and are adept at blaming others for their behavior.

The difference between NPD and a narcissistic personality style has to do with an individual's degree of internal shame. Shame is sometimes called the "sickness of the soul," and it's the core emotion that narcissists try to avoid. Narcissists spend their lives trying to overcome or eradicate the pervasive infection of shame that they feel. In fact, most of their abhorrent behaviors derive from their desire to rid themselves of shame. Unfortunately, this means transferring the shame to someone close to them: an employee, coworker, or more commonly, a child or a spouse/partner. (Hotchkiss, 2003)

Shame, often experienced during childhood and early adolescence, is the relentless driver of pathological narcissism. One individual with NPD described this shame as living with the monsters that are seen in the dark of every child's bedroom. The possibility of a light being turned on and exposing these monsters or the danger of public exposure to this shame is intolerable. In order to avoid this pervasive shame, a person with NPD will lie, withdraw, rage, and desperately feed the illusion of the grandiose self. This is a pattern of behavior that was adopted as a child to survive the anguish of not being heard, seen, or comforted. These wounds are so ingrained and the defenses so strongly entrenched that the man or woman with NPD will avoid exposing their vulnerability. Ironically it's only through exposing vulnerability that an individual with NPD can change.

Contrast this with situational narcissism. This type of narcissistic style can occur when people fall under the influence of power and fame. Anyone from movie stars to doctors, lawyers, and politicians can be pushed into the limelight and suddenly have fans worshiping them as if they were gods. They may end up behaving like pathological narcissists when it comes to the expectation of special treatment and the craving for unquenchable adoration. Another example of narcissistic traits can be found in addicts or alcoholics who, while using, may destroy anyone or anything standing in the way of feeding their addictions. But whether a movie star or an addict, people with narcissistic traits can feel remorse while those with NPD do not. As a result, people with narcissistic traits might also have this internal sense of shame, but their potential for recovery and relational healing is more promising than those with NPD. That's because people with narcissistic traits often have the capacity to recognize their behaviors, see how they impact others, and do the work necessary to move from reactivity to healing.

Narcissistic Personality Disorder	Narcissistic Personality Style
React to criticism with feelings of rage, stress, or humiliation	Hypersensitive to negative assessments, but display a willingness to change
Exploitative, take advantage of others	Shrewd in dealing with others but capacity to demonstrate fairness
Grandiose sense of self-importance, entitlement, masking emptiness	Sell themselves by lying, manipulation, or effusive charm
Preoccupied with fantasies of unlimited success, power, brilliance, beauty, or love	Talk about being the "best" in their field; but able to register the internal emotion of shame
Demand that others treat them with adoration and respect regardless of their behavior	An expectation that a relationship will meet their needs without any reciprocity. Resentful of having to give in relationships

Narcissistic Personality Disorder	Narcissistic Personality Style
Lack empathy: unable to recognize and experience how others feel	Some awareness of the feelings of others, but preoccupied with their own emotions
Inability to feel or express remorse	Can feel remorse, guilt, and shame, but guard against feeling these emotions
Require years of treatment, and prognosis for change is minimal	Often accompanies addiction or compulsive disorders. Prognosis is more hopeful

PATHOLOGICAL NARCISSISM

A pathological narcissist—that is, someone with NPD—is characterized less by traits like grandiosity, arrogance, or hypersensitivity than by his or her severely disturbed relationships. The characteristics of entitlement, grandiosity, contempt, and even joyful cruelty make it literally impossible to have life-giving connections with others. Yet this state often goes unrecognized, even by therapists. When the children and spouses of narcissists become aware of the dynamics of this devastating disorder, they experience both pain and relief. At last, someone recognizes what living in hell has been like for them. Many have a sense that they've been in prison, and it can take them a lifetime to comprehend how their captivity could have been so dangerous and yet so compelling.

Many people mistakenly believe that narcissism is really about individuals who feel superior. But the truth is that a genuine narcissist has no sense of self. They're desperate for praise because it's the closest they'll ever get to unconditional love. (Vaknin, 2007) Think of a narcissist as the equivalent of an addict when it comes to the need for adoration or attention. Without the adoring, attentive reflection of others, narcissists feel as if they don't exist. Worse, they feel intense humiliation and disgust for themselves. You'd never guess this by their behavior. In fact, it's because of their grandiose behavior that others eventually revile them.

A true narcissist cannot allow others to affect him in any way. When you can't allow others to have any impact on you, the result is a disconnection from others and the devastating lack of well-being that a relationship provides. Narcissists don't necessarily think they're better than other people; they just don't think of people at all. (Bernstein, 2002) They behave as if the world exists primarily for their gratification, and people exist only as pawns that allow them to direct their self-centered dramas.

When relating to a narcissist, it's important to remember that the behaviors we've discussed here are related directly to childhood trauma. They are survival mechanisms that were formed in sadistic environments among other narcissists who learned the same survival skills in their childhoods. These defense mechanisms are passed down through the generations and systematically choke the life out of children. Narcissistic parents beget narcissistic children.

Everyone Is a Little Narcissistic

*T*here are times when all of us become self-indulgent and immature. Perhaps the best way to understand this type of narcissism is to think of a two-year-old. For all their charm, toddlers are unable to see the world from anyone else's perspective but their own. If they don't get what they want, they throw their rattle out of the crib. It's quite natural behavior and programmed into all humans. This developmental narcissism is what Freud called primary narcissism. As we get older, through the influence of parents and others, most of us lose that self-indulgent streak to some extent. We learn that there are consequences to our actions and that we must take into account the needs of others if we are to find fulfillment and happiness. (Crompton, 2007)

All of us know how it feels to revert to this primary narcissism when we're feeling upset, because it protects us from further hurt. For instance, if you are fired from a job or irritated with a coworker, you may take the position that you're better than the rest of them and may even look down on others verbally or in silence. Or, if you have a breakup with someone you love, you may try to boost your ego by stating, "I was too good for her and she knows it."

Today, however, people have moved beyond occasional primary narcissism and come to believe that they are *entitled*—that they have a right to live life and have relationships totally on their own terms. But no relationship is "free." Constraints and responsibilities are integral to human interaction. (Solomon, 1992) Still, the normal need for autonomy and differentiation has, for some, been distorted into an attitude of self above all. Cultural messages all around us confirm this self-centered approach to living. Even popular magazines reflect this in a succession of titles ranging from *People* to *Us* to *Self*. The next one will probably be a periodical called *Me!*

When the focus of life is on determining one's own needs and finding someone who can fill those needs, any relationship is in danger of being destroyed by narcissistic expectations. Unfortunately there are those who have adopted a quasi-spiritual view of love as another way to meet their own needs while pretending to enhance the "greater good." I'm referring to New Age rhetoric that encourages us to embrace all of humanity, but, ironically, no one in particular.

A NATION OF BABIES

"You're only young once,
but you can be immature forever."

—GERMAINE GREER

The majority of parents in this country are not affluent, but we live in an affluent culture. And just as poverty has a profound influence on us, so too does affluence. It can create marvelous opportunities as well as long-lasting problems such as spoiled children with obnoxious behavior and superior attitudes, unmotivated adolescents who care only for their video games, and reckless teenagers living delinquent and self-destructive lives. The end result may be a kind of endless adolescence.

Many claim that narcissism is a cultural disorder. Cell phones and the instant availability of cash and almost any consumer good your heart desires promote fragility by weakening self-regulation. "You get used to things happening right now and right away," says psychologist Bernardo J. Carducci of the University of Indiana. "You not only want the pizza now, you generalize that expectation to friendship and intimate relationships. You become frustrated and impatient easily. You become unwilling to work out problems." (Carducci, 2000)

There is a belief that far too many children in America are being overindulged and showered with excess material goods. While not all parents who raise narcissists are themselves narcissistic, overindulgent parenting is the formula for producing entitled children. Before I explain this, let me be clear about the notion of spoiling children. I don't think that infants can be spoiled enough. There comes a time, however, when parents need to use structure, limits, and boundaries. If they don't, their children may become immoral, contemptuous, and self-obsessed.

There are often mitigating circumstances driving an overindulgent parenting style. Some parents who grew up with scarcity want to give their children all that money can buy. Working mothers and fathers may feel compelled to lavish their children with material goods in payment for their absence. Some parents can't tolerate their children's uncomfortable emotions and, in order to soothe themselves, they indulge their children. But this prevents their kids from learning how to work through emotions and acquire important developmental skills. For instance, shame is a normal developmental phenomenon in childhood. Healthy shame is important because without it, we lose the distinct senses of discretion, tact, and conscience. Healthy shame manifests in emotions like humility and embarrassment—emotions that promote good socialization (and prevent us from running naked to the grocery store). Children must be allowed to experience discomfort in order to develop a conscience.

One of the most consistent findings in a study conducted on adults from overindulgent families showed that subjects attributed overindulgence to abuse and neglect. (Allison, 2000) Statistically, there are high levels of physical and psychological violence in households where overindulgence occurs. Overindulgence also appears related to chemical dependency, death of a family member, illness, or other medical issues. When one parent is not functioning because of one of these situations, there can be a guilt-ridden drive to compensate children by lavishing them with gifts and indulging their bad behavior. Guilt is a prime motivator in overindulging a child. This emotion pushes parents to cater to their children's tantrums and whims. Parents wind up shifting their boundaries and compromising their integrity to ease their remorse—completely unaware of the damage they are inflicting.

We are all self-centered to some extent. Narcissism is on a continuum, and some people clearly have more of a problem than others. M. Scott Peck was one of the first popular writers to address this topic. He later said, "My own view is that we are all born narcissists. With the help of parents we grow out of it. However, if childhood is far from ideal the essential immaturity of narcissism is never left behind." (Peck, 2003)

In our culture, we are pushed to conform to societal norms of success. We're told what to wear, how to act, what's chic and what's not, and that only women who fit into a size two are beautiful. From magazines to newspapers, every form of media dictates what we need to look like in order to feel good about ourselves. Most people are not immune to this media barrage and become slaves to the images that are projected. As we surrender to this pressure, we become eternally dissatisfied.

Being one's true self takes both tremendous courage and humility. It means knowing one's limits and boundaries, and maintaining them. It means looking into the mirror and seeing ourselves as we are.

WHAT IS OVERINDULGENT PARENTING?

Parents who give children too much, too soon, for too long, and at developmentally inappropriate times can be considered overindulgent. These parents overindulge to meet their *own* needs, not the needs of their children, and they deprive their kids from completing important developmental tasks. Overweening, smothering, spoiling, overvaluing, and idolizing the child are all forms of parental abuse. Pioneering psychologist Karen Horney points out why: "The child is dehumanized and instrumentalized. His parents love him not for what he really is—but for what they wish and imagine him to be: the fulfillment of their dreams and frustrated wishes." (Horney, 1991)

It's interesting that adults who consider themselves overindulged as children say that this excessive style produced both negative and positive feelings. Such ambivalent and inconsistent feelings are difficult for children to interpret and lead to feelings of insecurity and chaos (Sroufe, Fox & Pancake, 1993). It's no surprise that as adults, these indulged children internalize statements like these: "I need praise and material reward to feel worthy." "I don't have to grow up because other people will take care of me." "I feel like I need lots of things to feel good about myself." "I am unlovable."

What is just as disturbing is that these same adults are much more likely to overindulge themselves and their own children compared to nonindulged adults. So the cycle of overindulgence, entitlement, and narcissism goes on.

I recently met a fourteen-year-old girl named Ellie who came from an upper middle-class family. The mother was busy with social functions, and her father was a sex addict who had a business to run, which kept him away from home for the majority of each month. When Mom couldn't cope with her daughter's moods, she determined that it was time to hire a personal assistant to manage her teenager's affairs. Mom then didn't have to bother with the details of Ellie's world and could deal with her ongoing investigation of her husband's activities as well as do the fundraising events that were a priority for her.

When I was about to meet this girl, I received a call from her personal assistant requesting a meeting. A teenager's personal assistant has never called me, and I was confused about who, exactly, was showing up for the appointment! Before I agreed to see Ellie, I requested a session with her mother. Her mother agreed to a phone conversation and proceeded to use this time to complain about her husband and pick my brain about a good therapist for him. When I tried to ascertain the reason for Ellie to be in therapy, Mom got teary and felt remorse for not spending enough time with her, but she blamed it on her husband's sex addiction. "She doesn't have any friends," the mother cried, "and I just want her to be happy."

When Ellie came for her appointment, she was depressed and appeared bored and angry. She had been shunned by other kids her age and felt as if she had to buy her friendships by giving expensive gifts and extravagant trips on her father's yacht. Despite her attempts at buying friends, she also felt quite entitled to treat them badly. Finally her friends became impatient with her and found her overbearing. Her neediness took the form of extremely demanding behavior that pushed people away.

During therapy, Ellie revealed her deep pain and isolation at home. "Dad's always preoccupied with someone else, and Mom is always preoccupied with Dad." Ellie naturally internalized her parents' inattention and evaluated herself as ugly, boring, uninteresting, and as she put it, terminally "gross." Ellie was aware of her shame, but her feelings of anger and entitlement weren't far behind. One day Ellie was thirty-five minutes late for her appointment, and I let her know we only had a short time for a session that day.

"That's no problem," she said. "I'll just pay you extra and we can just go on." When I mentioned that I had someone else coming in, she raised her offer of money as if she were bidding on an item for auction. When she finally understood that I wasn't going to change my appointment for her, she stood up, told me that her mother would hear about this, and slammed the door. Her personal secretary called the next day and let me know that Ellie had found another therapist with a better reputation, and she would no longer need my services.

The price of overindulgence, particularly as a substitute for human connection, is tragic. Hopefully Ellie got the help she needed. If not, she'll never be able to trust that another person can love her, just for who she is.

Helicopter Parenting

The helicopter parent is the one who waits for a signal and then swoops in to rescue the child. Helicopter parents send a message that their children are fragile and can't make it without them. (Cline & Fay, 2006) The motivation behind this parental behavior is an inability or unwillingness to tolerate their children's discomfort. Unfortunately it is disguised as loving a child so much that the parent is willing to do anything for them (and therefore keep their own "guts" quiet).

Helicopter parents are those over-the-top moms and dads who follow their children to college—staying a week, two, or even more to get them settled. *Fast Company,* a magazine that reports on technology and industry, reports that "parents now accompany their children to their first job, demanding respect and raises even if their darlings aren't meeting their numbers." This unfortunate dynamic creates a population of adults who not only cannot cope with their own emotions but who cannot withstand the challenges and vicissitudes of life. Having every whim gratified has the effect of prolonging infantile narcissism, and the child develops a social handicap with very little capacity for mutual interaction, cooperation, sharing, and empathic understanding. Growing up with the expectation that others are there to meet their needs, these children feel entitled to remain unencumbered by responsibility. When they inevitably run into difficulty, children of "helicopter parents" tend to blame others for their behavior, primarily their parents.

Whenever I speak to audiences about narcissism, I always ask for a show of hands from those who grew up in what they consider to be a healthy family. At first, there are quite a few confused expressions followed by the question: "What is a healthy family?" In the last few decades we've focused so much on dysfunction that some don't really know what healthy means.

I'm reminded of a cartoon that depicts a convention for adults from normal families with only one person in attendance. To understand the etiology of narcissism, it's helpful to have a basic template for healthy parenting.

The Phenomenon of Healthy Parenting

*I*t is essential for parents to understand that there is a difference between nurture, structure, and overindulgence. Nurture is unconditional love, and it's an essential part of children's growth and well-being. But unconditional love is not enough. Children also need to learn limits, skills, and standards. That's where structure comes in. Providing structure requires parents to set healthy boundaries and limits with children. There always needs to be a healthy balance between nurturing and structuring. Overindulgence is misguided nurturing and inadequate structuring.

Parenting experts Jean Clarke and Connie Dawson describe this exquisite balance as the ability to parent with love and logic: "When you parent with love and logic, you learn to love in healthy ways and effectively guide your children without resorting to anger, threats, power struggles, and rescuing that will haunt them along the path to adulthood. And, children will learn responsibility and the logic of life by solving their own problems and acquiring the tools they'll need to cope with the real world." (Clarke & Dawson, 1998)

For the most part, parents do the best they can with the tools they have. No parent wakes up in the morning deciding they will strip their child of dignity and self-respect. But with the onset of terrorism, sexually transmitted diseases, and easy access to pornography and drugs, parents are challenged beyond their capabilities. Unfortunately, the result is either overprotection or not enough protection. The following are suggestions for ways to avoid raising entitled and overindulged children:

1. Never invest more in an outcome than your child does.
2. Resist the urge to schedule your child in a way that allows little free time. Children of all ages need time for free play in order to learn social skills, self-regulation, and cognitive skills.
3. Be reasonable about what is dangerous and what is not dangerous. (Some of these fears may be yours and not realistic.)
4. Allow your child to tolerate discomfort. Don't overreact to every bad grade or negative encounter your child has. Sometimes discomfort is the appropriate response to a situation and a stimulus to self-improvement.
5. Modify your expectations about child raising in light of your child's temperament; the same actions don't work with everyone.
6. Recognize that there are many paths to success. If we impose our dreams on our children and try to fit them into a particular mode, it's a setup for failure.
7. Don't manipulate the academic system on behalf of your child; it makes kids feel guilty and doubtful of their own ability.
8. Remember that the goal of child rearing is to raise independent adults. Encourage your children to think for themselves, to disagree respectfully with authority,

and even to endure the critical gaze of their peers. (Furstenberg 2006)

HEALTHY NARCISSISM

Healthy narcissism involves the right to feel satisfied, special, and unique; to be the best you can be; to accomplish, win, and be celebrated; to be acknowledged and to be the center of attention; and to expect attention, respect, and support when asked for and needed. A sense of entitlement can also be a critical motivational force in a person's personal and professional development. Entitlement serves an important part in normal self-esteem regulation. In pathological narcissism, however, entitlement is exaggerated and associated with boastful grandiosity that serves to modulate underlying feelings of inferiority, shame, and rage. The following stories will give you an example of healthy versus unhealthy entitlement:

Seven-year-old Kathy reminded her father at breakfast that he forgot to say good night to her the night before and told him that she felt sad and mad. The father apologized, explained that he had been doing the taxes, gave her an extra morning hug, and promised that he would not forget to say good night to her that evening.

—∿—

Another child, seven-year-old Susan, whose mother also forgot to say good night the night before because she was drunk at her daughter's bedtime, did not remind her mother next morning. She assumed that her mother was not feeling well, and she had learned from past experiences with her mother's irritable reactions not to intrude when her mother needed to be alone.

While Kathy obviously expected her father to acknowledge her feelings and reactions, Susan's sense of emotional entitlement was much more compromised. Ironically, it's Susan who is much more susceptible to developing destructive entitlement as she grows older. Why? Unhealthy entitlement comes from unmet emotional needs. Because Susan's basic needs have been met with irritation, she's learned to connect her needs with shame. This girl has learned to throw her needs in the garbage in order to take care of an alcoholic mother. Thus, when her needs arise, she'll feel a deep wound that will trigger entitlement and anger or disconnection and self-abuse. Her hunger for attachment combined with her shame is a potent neurochemical cocktail for addiction and compulsive behavior.

Healthy narcissism is healthy self-regard. It is the experience of being loved by others as well as having one's love returned. Healthy narcissism propels us to choose another person with the aim of being loved by that person. Healthy narcissism plays a crucial role in the human capacity to manage challenges, successes, and changes; to overcome defeats, illnesses, trauma, and losses; to love and be productive and creative; and to experience satisfaction and acceptance about the course of one's life. Healthy narcissism is the base of healthy self-esteem, feelings, and relationships. The inability to love is a source of inferiority feelings.

PARENTING SUGGESTIONS: BREAKING THE "YOU OWE ME" SYNDROME

How do parents assist children to grow out of their natural narcissistic stage and yet foster healthy entitlement? The following statements may help launch children of all ages into a healthier version of narcissism. It's always a challenge for parents to tolerate the difficult emotions of their children, especially as they go through this predictable stage of narcissism. When children throw age-inappropriate tantrums or display deep sadness, some parents offer gifts, food, or other placebos because it's so difficult to see your child in pain. This may be well intentioned, but fosters grandiosity and entitlement. When a child or adolescent is acting as if they have the right to be abusive, disrespectful, or receive privileges, it's important that parents display a firm, yet gentle approach; and since this stage of development is so tricky, it's good to be prepared with some age-appropriate options. The following statements may help launch children of all ages into a healthier version of narcissism:

"You feel that your needs aren't being met. When you can respectfully tell me about that, I'd like to listen."

"When I was younger, I used to get angry when what I was really feeling was hurt. Is that true for you? I'll be glad to talk to you more about that when you're ready."

"What is our rule about buying you things every time we go out? You can learn to feel good inside without having to have new toys all the time. What else makes you feel good?"

"I know this is important to you, but I want to explain something. Big deals are parents screaming at you, hitting you, leaving you, or having nasty fights around you. 'Little deals' are not getting your own way. You don't have to get angry over little deals."

"Using the car is a privilege and not an automatic right that you have. If you're going to disobey the rules of the house, then this privilege is taken away. It's up to you."

"It's sad to see a smart person like you making yourself so angry all the time. Some people talk about feelings so they don't have to get angry so much. I wonder if you could do that?"

"You get angry when I don't give you what you want. The truth is that none of us always get what we want. I know that's a hard lesson to learn."

"When someone doesn't respond to you the way that you want, you become angry. You are smart enough to know that doing this isn't going to change anything. You have the power to feel good even though you don't always get your way."

"You keep insisting that I buy you things. I wonder why you want to argue instead of doing things that would make you happy?"

"If you'd like to make requests instead of demands, I'll talk to you. If you're going to continue to have a tantrum, I'll have to leave the room until you calm down."

"You used to take care of the hard feelings inside by insisting that you get your own way. That doesn't work anymore. What can you do now instead of blowing up?"

"When you neglect your responsibilities you are making a choice. I'm not willing to support these choices. You can get as angry as you'd like, but I'm not going to rescue you from the consequences of your behavior."

When a child is given the opportunity to struggle with their emotions and is fortunate enough to have a parent who is willing to listen to their needs without necessarily indulging them, then healthy narcissism can emerge. No one knows conclusively how narcissistic personality disorder develops; however, parents have a powerful role in ameliorating destructive narcissistic traits in their children. Of course, there are situations and temperaments over which we have no control. The following chapter will explain some of these factors as well as the origins of narcissism.

5

*H*ow the Narcissistic Personality Is Formed

*T*he exact cause of narcissistic personality disorder is unknown, but researchers have identified childhood developmental factors, parenting behaviors, and neurobiological factors that may contribute to the disorder:

- Overindulgence and overvaluation by parents.
- Valued by parents as a means to regulate their own self-esteem.
- Excessive admiration that is never balanced with realistic feedback.
- Unpredictable or unreliable caregiving from parents.
- Severe emotional abuse in childhood.
- Continuous praise by adults for perceived exceptional looks or talents.
- Learning manipulative behaviors from parents.
- Deficits in the development of right brain activity.
- Overstimulation of autonomic nervous system.

Trust and love are the foundations of life-giving relationships. All we know about ourselves comes from the way people loved us. This is so vital that it determines whether we feel esteemed and valued or worthless and hateful. Those who don't have a sense of internal value have been taught by the failure of the way people loved them. Every family passes on a legacy of love and trust through the generations. Parents who received an adequate supply of quality love and trust are in turn able to hand down the same to their children. When parents did not receive enough love and trust, they struggle to give these essentials to their offspring. Thus one generation of scarcity begets another.

When people experience violations of love they often vacillate between feelings of rage and shame.

> **Rage:** "You owed me love. You're monsters. How could you have responded to me like that? I detest you."
>
> **Shame:** "They were right. I'm not lovable. I deserved what I got."

The quality of trustworthiness informs us if people are going to give us what we need or take advantage of us. Learning this important characteristic teaches children what they need to do in order to get along with others, and it has a direct effect on how we behave in relationships. If we felt unsafe as children, if we were manipulated or abused, then we experienced violations of trustworthiness. The responses to violations of trust are control and/or chaos:

> **Control:** "Do it my way on my timetable. If you don't, I'm out of here."
>
> **Chaos:** "Life is going to screw you anyway. It's going to get you, so why bother?"

(If an individual vacillates between rage, shame, control, and chaos, they most likely have either a borderline personality disorder or a narcissistic personality disorder.) (Bosnormeny-Nagy 1984)

When trustworthiness is extinguished, children develop the belief that they have to struggle to get what they deserve. These children no longer trust parents to give them what they need, so they withdraw, manipulate, threaten, verbally abuse, and feel little if any remorse doing so. This is called *destructive entitlement:* the greenhouse for narcissistic grandiosity, entitlement, and disregard for others. Thus, there is a lack of conscience as these children make certain decisions: "No one is there. No one really cares. I will to do whatever it takes to get my needs met, no matter what the cost to others."

THE TRAGIC EQUATION: INADEQUATE REFLECTION + ABANDONMENT FEAR = ENTITLEMENT, SHAME, TORMENT, AND RAGE

Two ingredients are necessary for children to develop into emotionally healthy human beings: mirroring and object constancy. There are no perfect parents, and not one of us gets a perfect grade in flawless mirroring and unwavering constancy. However, many parents are too preoccupied with their own pain to give their children an ample dose of these essential ingredients for emotional health.

Mirroring

From infancy onward, it's a parent's job to provide their children with a clear mirror of who they are. This is done through sight, sound, and touch by caregivers who are present for their children instead of being consistently preoccupied with their own issues. "Reflection" is the process through which parents mirror children's essence back to them. It's through this mirroring that children develop a sense of their own identity.

For instance, when parents imitate a baby's sounds or movements, it's often clear that the child is delighted. In those precious moments the child is the beneficiary of warmth, focused attention, and admiration. As children grow, simple statements like, "Hello, blue eyes!" or "I can see that you really like to eat," and even "You can say *no* better than anybody!" are examples of reflection. A child's identity is shaped through eye contact, touch, and sound. When children receive this kind of reflection, they develop a sense of who they are.

In order to provide healthy mirroring, parents have to be present, bear witness, and reflect back to their child. However, when a parent's own trauma, wounds, or unmet needs override their ability to be present to a child, the child's core sense of self can be lost, fragmented, or undeveloped. (Marks, 2007) Parents with distorted or cloudy mirrors leave children desperate for self-definition. Children can sense when a parent is preoccupied and as they grow, these same children will need to depend on others to "know" who they are. They will be desperate for mirroring, and their identity will depend on the reflection they get back from people around them (which, as we know, can change from minute to minute).

When this child becomes an adult and gets into a relationship, she won't understand why it's so excruciating when perfect mirroring isn't available from the one she loves. For a narcissist, their identity is so fragile or nonexistent that if a loved one thinks they're beautiful, they'll bask in that reflection and treat the partner like a god or goddess. If, however, the narcissist gets the slightest hint of disapproval from her mate, she may treat him vindictively and abusively.

This need for mirroring will inevitably spill over to other areas of life. This can translate into the "high maintenance" employee who needs so much affirmation and approval that it becomes exhausting. Supervisors or colleagues are skillfully manipulated into giving this affirmation for fear of angry outbursts and underhanded retaliation.

Tragically, the worst scenario ensues if narcissists have children. The kids feel responsible for their parent's sense of self. In other words, instead of the parent providing children with clear mirroring, the reverse will be true. This dynamic drains a child and makes him feel empty. On the other hand, this process is precisely what passes narcissism from one generation to another. Can you imagine how falsely empowering this would be for a child? To be five years old and feel responsible for a parent's esteem is a very grandiose experience! This is the breeding ground for narcissistic tendencies that unfortunately get passed down from generation to generation. (Lerner, 1995) Narcissism can be seen as a simultaneous trauma to the core self as well as neglect/deprivation of the core self. While healthy mirroring feeds and reinforces the developing sense of self, narcissistic mirroring breaks down the boundaries of the developing self. With narcissistic mirroring, the developing self is lost, overshadowed, or never activated.

Object Constancy

Object constancy means the tendency for objects to be perceived as unchanging despite changes in the positions and conditions. (Think of the parent-child game "peekaboo" for instance.) Object constancy is the process through which a child develops a secure base. Whether a caregiver is in sight or not, whether a child is misbehaving or compliant, there will always be a constant caregiver who can be depended upon.

When a parent is consistent in attending to the needs of a child and following through emotionally and physically, the child acquires some core beliefs:

A basic trust in others as responsive.
Belief that the world is a benevolent place.
Confidence in being able to communicate needs.

Without this constancy a youngster will anticipate abandonment. Therefore, it will be difficult for this child to relate in an honest way to others because of the anticipation of inevitable loss. This expectation is so consuming that this child's entire set of beliefs and assumptions will be based on avoiding abandonment despair. Subsequently, she may become very vigilant in order to prevent becoming overwhelmed, making sure at all times that her environment and the people in it can be controlled. She'll become acutely aware of any nuance of inattention or neglect from a partner, friend, or coworker. Her antenna is so keen that any transition or sudden change results in severe anxiety, a profound sense of fear, and in some cases, rage. (Smith, 2007)

This is the recipe for a pervasive sense of defectiveness or shame. As she grows and notices other children interact with parents, this child develops a core belief that she must be inherently bad; otherwise, her own parents would give her the love and constancy she longs for. Tragically, she holds herself to blame for her parent's inadequacy and self-indulgence. This internal sense of defectiveness persists throughout life, and the goal of this child becomes getting rid of this hideous, intolerable emotion.

Another scenario exists when instead of engaging in anxious manipulation to insure a safe and secure environment, a narcissist develops this mindset: "If anyone is going to control the leaving around here, I am!" Since narcissists anticipate that abandonment is going to happen, they posture themselves so that they are in charge of the exit. In relationships, narcissists will provoke those around them to leave by being cruel, neglectful, or abusive. Or they will regularly threaten abandonment to make sure their partner stays adequately anxious and attentive to their needs.

Regardless of what reactions develop in childhood one quality remains constant: the formation of important core beliefs that cast a shadow over all future interactions. The development of a lack of conscience and no empathy is rooted in the defensive strategies of a child with little or no mirroring or constancy. At some point, this child makes three decisions that affect all her future relationships: "I'm going to play by my own rules now." "It's not safe to get close to people." "I'm never going to be hurt again."

The quality of mirroring and constancy that a child receives will determine how he learns to attach to others. For instance, if a child is raised in an alcoholic family and gets love and attention intermittently, this young one will never quite know when he can expect to get nurturing and when it's going to disappear. Can we possibly comprehend this child's anxiety as he wonders from day to day if there will be a parent at home who is fully there? As an adult, he'll likely become anxious, clingy, demanding, or outraged when he detects any fluctuation in attention or admiration from others. This dynamic will also set up a child for addiction to drugs, sex, gambling, or relationships in order to medicate the pain of insecure, anxious attachments.

Parents can often feign warmth, but not closeness. Their children grow to detect this incongruity and become adept students at learning how to put on a show of love while feeling indifferent. As adults, these same children can turn on the charm and charisma, but can't emotionally connect deeply with others.

Narcissism develops as a child's spirit shuts down in early life. This can be due to trauma, a parent's total self-absorption, or a parent's over involvement in the child's life in ways that are suffocating and developmentally inappropriate. Any or all of these things can lead to the trauma of "attachment failure."

Traumatic experiences can shake the foundations of our beliefs about safety, and shatter our assumptions of trust. Francine Shapiro, a specialist in trauma recovery, differentiates between the terms "small t" and "large T" trauma. (Shapiro, 1998) While most people recognize the negative effects of extreme forms of trauma, such as abuse, violence, and crime, they may be unaware that seemingly benign childhood situations can lead to widespread and hidden aftereffects that are just as debilitating. The origins of small-"t" trauma lie in those unresolved moments, often in childhood, when you felt overwhelmed, powerless, and confused. The following are examples of "small t" traumas that reverberate throughout one's life and can lead to narcissistic entitlement, rage, and a profound sense of shame:

- The trauma of not being seen.
- The trauma of having needs and knowing they won't be met.
- The trauma of being alone with no one available for connection.
- The trauma of being in distress with no one available for comfort.

THE RAPPROCHEMENT PHASE
OF DEVELOPMENT

In some ways, adult narcissists can behave like two-year-olds having a tantrum. Ironically, there is now research that shows that narcissistic organization develops between fifteen months to twenty-five months of age. Alan Schore, a behavioral specialist and expert on the origins of personality disorders, says, "The hot flush of shame, or anger; the heavy ache of sadness, or loss: These physical sensations appear to activate areas in the brain that did not develop normally in narcissists' second year of life." (Schore, 1995) In understanding the etiology of narcissism, it's helpful to understand more about the neurological and psychological events during the rapprochement phase of development.

The rapprochement phase of development occurs around fifteen months of age when the child becomes aware of her separateness from the caregiver. The toddler experiences both the excitement of emerging independence and the fear of her vulnerability and dependence. There is a need for the caregiver to attune properly the child's excitement and vulnerability at that time. (Kohut, 1970; Mahler, 1979)

The terrible or terrific twos are challenging for any parent; however when a caregiver fails to attune to the child at this stage, the result is excessive shame combined with the sense that excitement is dangerous. In other words, the child cannot regulate this state of "excited shame," and the caregiver's response cannot provide the structure that teaches the child how to recover from shame.

Scientist Alan Schore and psychiatrist James Grotstein have speculated that narcissism may also have its roots in the undeveloped autonomic nervous system. (Schore 1994) In this rapprochement stage of development, the sympathetic and the parasympathetic nervous systems are still developing. (Think of the sympathetic nervous system as the "gas" and the parasympathetic nervous system as the "brakes.") Children during this stage of development cannot quite balance excitement with repose, fear with relaxation. The intense physiological state of shame distress reflects a sudden shift from sympathetic dominant to parasympathetic dominant autonomic nervous system activity. The child is thus propelled into a hypo-aroused affect state that she cannot yet autoregulate. It is postulated that narcissistic organization develops during this period when the child isn't given the structure to contain this excited sense of shame.

In addition, brain imaging studies suggest that deficits in the emotional connection between children and their primary caregiver at this stage affects the development of right-brain areas involved in empathy and compassion—something narcissists lack. This information combined with the study of psychodynamic theory (the systematized study and theory of the psychological forces that underlie human behavior) has exciting implications for the diagnosis and treatment of narcissistic personality disorder.

Although there are many theories on the etiology of narcissism, those that have the most potential in terms of diagnosis and treatment combine the psychological with the neurobiological. In truth, we are a complex mix of both. Integrating psychology and biology is an exciting paradigm shift in the way that psychologists understand narcissism (Schore, 1994).

Up to eighteen months of age, we have few words to describe internal emotions. If painful things are occurring in our lives, such as attachment failure, and we have few words to describe them, we grow up unable to express important things going on in our relationships. In other words, articulate as they may be, narcissists lack the ability to express vulnerability and authenticity in their relationships. Many lack the emotional intelligence and awareness to do so.

When any of the above occurs, a child will form a false sense of self to help avoid depression, abandonment, and the all-encompassing shame. The defenses of entitlement and selfishness keep a child from feeling vulnerable and unworthy. The defense of entitlement helps keep a child from the unbearable belief of "I am bad" that may have developed when he felt parental rejection and feared abandonment early in life. This child's secret conviction becomes, "I am defective, or my parents would have loved me." This belief persists throughout life, and remembering early painful experiences of hurt and shame are avoided at all costs. (Namka, 1997)

ORIGINS OF THE NARCISSISTIC WOUND

A poignant depiction of narcissistic parenting can be seen in the movie *Shine*. It's the true story of a musically gifted young man and his narcissistically wounded father. Even though the father has devoted his life to the development of his son's music, he forbids his son to take true ownership of his talents. The tragic outcome of such a double bind is for the son to go mad. In the film, we are allowed to share in the adult son's journey back to selfhood. In the end, he's able to reclaim his music as his own and recognize that his relationship with his father is beyond all hope.

When a parent's own wounds, unmet needs, or undeveloped self render them unable to be present for a child and respond to their vulnerable needs, the child's core sense of self is affected. An underdeveloped core sense of self is the root of the narcissistic wound. Raw, broken, undeveloped, and lost, narcissists enter a cold cruel world ill-equipped to relate and connect with the spirit of life. A narcissistic wound is a reflection of a parent's failure to give their child a sense of dignity, love, respect, worth, esteem, concern, and trust.

This wound creates emotional birth defects that stunt the capacity to be fully human and program narcissists for relational failure. In this sense, the narcissistic defense is a natural result of the response to trauma. Here, trauma is defined as an interpersonal violation of the boundaries of the self, which may be fragile to start with. This trauma also includes elements of deprivation and neglect. (Marks, 2007)

We sometimes refer to the narcissistic wound as the "emptiness wound." (Almaas, 2004) Narcissistic parents pass on the narcissistic wound through their own lack of a grounded sense of self, their unclear or broken boundaries, and their inability to be present or respond to the needs of a developing child. (Marks, 2007)

Children of narcissistic parents carry a vague sense of dread about the underlying dark emotional wound. In time, that wound becomes the source of immense terror as it opens to shame and emptiness.

As these children reach their adulthood, their hypersensitivity to neglect or criticism becomes acute. When narcissists feel threatened and in danger of losing their sense of omnipotence or superiority, they feel as if they're dropping into an abyss. They are "reduced to size" and open to feeling shame. When special treatment from others evaporates, it causes an emotional injury that's so devastating it must be avoided at all costs. To escape the intolerable emotions of shame and despair, the narcissist tries to dodge this pain by manipulating and even doing harm to others.

The three usual reasons for a narcissistic injury are:

- threat of the losing the primary source of admiration or attention;
- some failure in which old strategies no longer work;

- a situation where their robust sense of self dissolves and they become desperate.

When a wound is triggered, narcissists often act in one of three ways:
- desperately grope for alternative sources of admiration and attention;
- become enraged, depressed, and/or childlike;
- self-medicate with drugs/alcohol.

NARCISSISTIC PARENTS

A colleague of mine once described her experience in growing up with narcissistic parents. She explained how she was praised when she was useful and cast aside and devalued when she was not. At the end of her explanation she turned to me and said, "Rokelle, narcissitic parents eat their young. Then we're supposed to be eternally grateful for their meal."

Narcissistic parents need everyone to believe that they are the most loving and nurturing parents in the universe—and many times, their children believe them. The children of narcissists may remain fiercely loyal to their parents because they hope someday to win their admiration and love. In my practice, I've even heard adult children of narcissistic parents say: "My mother and father were saints!" Actually, it's come to the point that whenever I hear such statements, I prepare for the worst. The reason is that the truth often turns out to be exactly the opposite.

NARCISSISTIC MOTHERS

"If it's not one thing . . . it's your mother."

—GEORGE CARLIN'S INTERPRETATION OF FREUD

Historically, Freud and other analysts attributed the root of narcissistic behavior to faulty empathy on the mother's part. Before I begin this section, it's important to remember that research on personality disorders such as narcissism has historically been conducted based on men's experiences. Add to this the fact that women have had the primary or sole responsibility for childrearing, and there is an obvious skewing of interpretation here. Thankfully, there are social movements today that promote increased responsibility by fathers as well as the phenomenon of the "house husband" who provides primary care and nurturing to children. But neither is a common occurrence.

It doesn't bode well for either gender when we place the responsibility of a child's psychological health on the mother, or focus on the mother-child bond as the source of emotional health or sickness. I'm not denying that this bond is important, but if we continue to lay this responsibility on the mother, we'll continue to develop males who need to defend their ego boundaries against women and to deny their strong relational needs. In addition, we'll continue to see women who attempt to locate their missing sense of self-esteem through merger with and dependency on others. (Chodorow & Philipson, 1992)

I also want to emphasize that all parents feel exhausted, depleted, and overwhelmed by the responsibilities of parenthood at times. I don't know of parents who have not done things they regret or have not had thoughts and feelings about their children that were anything but kind. This does not define them as narcissistic. The crucial difference in a narcissistic parent is the inability to show empathy or compassion for their children. These parents are so self-involved that they are unable to respond to their children's needs. Their primary goal is to be worshiped by their perfect offspring.

Pregnancy

Depending on emotional or financial circumstances, many women can become either detached from or overly invested in their pregnancy. One difference in narcissistic women, however, is that they become overwhelmingly preoccupied with their own experience rather than focused on the infant who will soon emerge. (Hotchkiss, 2003) For women who are somatic narcissists, every little ache or pain becomes a dramatic event. And, as their bodies change, they become increasingly anxious and fearful that their primary sources of supply will disappear. As a result, they may put themselves and their child at jeopardy by overexercising or undereating in order to medicate their fears and maintain their glamour.

A cerebral narcissistic woman may be so disconnected from her body during pregnancy that she may ignore signs or symptoms that indicate her baby may be in trouble. She will see her pregnancy as a nuisance that needs to be endured and thus may not nourish herself properly, or she might ignore prenatal care instructions, or continue on a stressful and strenuous daily routine that is not in the baby's best interests. Since a cerebral narcissist frequently dislikes her own body and dresses in ways that hide her figure, others may not be aware that she's even pregnant until the last trimester.

I would be remiss if I didn't also include here the narcissistic female addict who, because of the nature of the addictive disease, systematically destroys herself and her fetus. Fetal alcohol syndrome (FAS) and fetal alcohol effect (FAE), for example, are among the most preventable birth defects. Tragically, narcissistic addicts under the influence put their drug of choice above their unborn child or any other human attachment.

Infancy and Childhood

Newborns require a kind of selfless care that is typically more than a narcissistic woman can bear. If there is no way to escape the responsibilities, she may go through the motions with a mechanical indifference or negligence, unless, of course, others are watching. Then she'll give an award-winning performance of the perfect, doting mother. This addictive inconsistency not only leaves the child hungry for warmth, love, and attention, but also instills a core of defectiveness and shame over time.

A narcissistic mother ascribes adult meaning to a small child's behavior. She may become irritated and impatient with her child, and even demonize him. She fails to consider the child's age-appropriate needs and instead focuses on the price she pays for motherhood. It's not uncommon to hear a narcissistic mother claim that her infant is out to make her feel angry, crazy, or anxious on purpose: "This baby is so selfish. If he really cared about me he wouldn't cry when I'm talking on the phone." Or, if her toddler cannot carry out a particular task or can't perform for others in a way that feeds the mother's grandiosity, she may be warm and understanding in public but privately withhold love as a punishment.

On the other side of this spectrum, a narcissistic mother can become overinvolved and absorbed in her child to the extent that anything or anyone else in her life, including other children or her mate, goes unnoticed and neglected. Her "special" child may not be someone she can really love, but rather her pet project. Consequently she will restrict her child's autonomy, control him through shaming, and manipulate him in ways that resonate with her own narcissistic expectations. At the same time, she will inflate the child's sense of grandiosity and omnipotence because he is, after all, a reflection of her.

Since this mother cannot model empathy or contain

aggression, her child cannot master these important skills either. The result is a damaged, unrealistic self-concept and a personality that cannot defuse shame or ever quite learn how to give and receive love. In short, this is a breeding ground for a future narcissist or someone who will partner with a narcissist one day.

Gregory Bateson, a renowned anthropologist, social scientist and linguist, says, "Nature fills its vacuums. Mothering young children is exhausting and women need to have adult support as they go through the care of infants and toddlers. If a woman is partnered with a spouse who happens to be narcissistic and too self-absorbed to attend to her needs, through the course of time a mother may turn to the one supply of assured unconditional love, her child. The children who grow up with distancing narcissistic fathers and clinging narcissistic mothers pay a high price in their adulthood. The pall of unhealthy attachment casts a dark shadow on all their future relationships." (Bateson, 2002)

NARCISSISTIC FATHERS

Fathers are essential to their children's upbringing, and their masculine energy and perspective is important as children grow. Fathers have the key responsibility to teach their sons how to be men and their daughters how to relate to men. Fathers can be closely involved in the care and nurturing of children and can connect with them in intimate and powerful ways.

A narcissistic father, however, may not hide the fact that he did not intend to become a parent and may express bitterness for being tricked and manipulated into parenthood by a conniving female. From the beginning, a narcissistic father may abandon both mother and child and have very little interest in responsibilities like changing diapers, feeding, or getting up at two in the morning to comfort a small infant.

The father's resentment spills over to both the mother and the child. And even though it's not uncommon for males to feel left out of the symbiotic relationship between mother and child, this is when the narcissistic male feels perfectly entitled to go search for sex and intimacy elsewhere.

Contrast that to the narcissistic father who specializes in control and looks forward to the possibility of replicating himself. Rather than distancing from his child, he can dominate and mold his son or daughter to suit his needs. A dependent child is like a blank canvas that exists to create whatever image most pleases the narcissist. This father takes his children's reactions, successes, and failures quite personally. If a child comes home with a grade that's less than stellar, he or she will be subject to harsh punishment, an unending tirade, or cold, icy silence. Rather than being offered help, the child may get an earful of how disgraceful they are and how embarrassing it is that they can't achieve perfection.

From the child's infancy, this father may compete with his wife for the child's attention. In later years, he may compete with the child and enter into foolish, devastating, and sometimes risky challenges only to feed his insatiable ego. From aggressive sports, intellectual battles, or even dangerous competitions, narcissistic fathers can't resist the opportunities to remind their children who is king.

A classic example of this narcissistic competition is portrayed in the film *The Great Santini,* a story about an aging marine who runs his home like a military academy. During the course of this story, there comes a time during his son's adolescence when the father is showing his age and must prove his strength and superiority. He wakes his son in the middle of the night and insists that they play basketball in the pouring rain. When the son agrees and begins to win the game, this narcissistic father punches him in the stomach so violently that his son loses his breath and cries. Dad then cavalierly bounces the ball and makes several baskets. All the while, he's calling his son a "sissy" and a "faggot."

The violence and aggression that results from the bruised ego of a narcissist is terrifying. And while children are a primary source of supply, they also are the primary victims.

Children who are raised by narcissists leave home with unrealistic expectations coupled with the shame they felt when they couldn't measure up to their parent's standards. Yet there is a double bind that exists: as harsh and unloving as narcissistic parents may be, when they deign to smile upon you, it's as if the stars fell from the heavens; it's intense, it's absorbing, and it's addictive. Can you see how this intermittent and extraordinary experience propels these adult children to seek out this dynamic in another narcissistic man or woman?

Research shows that this is the most addictive bond there is. Consequently, as much as a child of a narcissist may loathe his parent and want to be nothing like the parent, the fierce loyalty to that parental figure persists. And the longing for those shining moments of approval drives them to choose people to love who will replicate that addictive, dramatic experience—like a narcissist. It's highly unlikely that children of narcissistic parents would choose someone who was raised in a healthy family; chances are that the boredom and lack of drama would drive them insane.

Adults who were raised by narcissists have been horribly betrayed. Their narcissistic parents have deceived them by following the three basic rules for raising a child *without* an internal sense of esteem:

1. Parents assume their child has nothing to say about the world, and what he or she does say is insignificant.
2. Parents assume their child has plenty to learn from them, but they have nothing to learn from their child.

3. Parents insist the child enter their world if they want contact. The parent, however, won't bother entering their child's world because it's unimportant.

Tragically, narcissistic parents see a child as an instrument to inflate their sense of self. So, connecting at the child's level is a waste of time. However, they can put on a performance of the "good parent" so that the world can admire them.

One of my clients, Ralph, told me that every year since he was eight, his father had promised to take him on a fishing trip for his tenth birthday. His dad was rarely home, and when he was, he was preoccupied and clearly not interested in his son's activities. Ralph held this dream of time alone with his Dad for two years. As his special birthday neared, Ralph remembers his father boasting to his friends and clients how he and his boy were going to have some bonding time. Ralph's excitement was all consuming as he told his friends and teachers about this event.

When the day came and they arrived at the fishing lodge, his dad's friends were all waiting for him to join them in the bar for a few beers. The upshot of this trip was that Ralph spent no time alone with his father and never did learn to fish. When the ten-year-old complained, his father raged: "How many boys do you think have a chance to go to places like this? You better show some appreciation, young fellow, or I'm never taking you anywhere again!" Dad slammed the door of their room and went to join his pals at the bar. Ralph followed him downstairs, only to witness his father imitating his behavior to his friends at the bar and portraying Ralph as a whining, infantile idiot.

Perhaps you can see the deviousness of this father's assault. When a narcissist goes into attack mode, it's usually hidden under the pretext of righteous punishment, advice, or, sometimes, manipulative praise. Not only that, but as in Ralph's case, the narcissistic parent will mutilate his child's feelings and then have no qualms about entertaining others at the child's expense. In short, Ralph's father's message is similar to that of all narcissistic parents: "If you can't meet my needs, you're expendable and of no value to me."

How do children respond to this type of parenting? They know that they're not being heard or seen, and as a result they see their world as unfair. They're not mirrored at home and there is no consistency except disappointment. Some of these children compensate on the playground and bully classmates in order to exercise their voice and power. Others grow up to be "successful" bullies, stepping on people all the way to the top. Others may use their beauty and charm to entrap their victims and use them until they no longer serve their purpose. Others, particularly girls, actively shut their parents out and may preoccupy themselves with the only part of the world in which they have a say: their own bodies. What to eat and what not to eat seem the only options available to them. Teenage eating disorders and the absence of nurturing go hand in hand.

Although children are primary targets, it matters very little to the narcissist where their source of adoration and attention comes from, as long as the supply is continual. The stress and high maintenance of keeping a narcissist 'fed' over time is more than any human can endure.

The Care and Feeding
of Narcissists

I lie compulsively and needlessly, all the time,
about everything. And, I often contradict myself.
I need to do this to make myself interesting or attractive.
In other words, I always need someone to provide me
with attention, admiration, and adulation.

—ALBERT BROOKS, COMEDIAN, ACTOR

*W*hen Bram Stoker wrote his famous legend of
Dracula, he adapted this character from a man in
his life who embodied the characteristics of a
narcissist. How apropos! The legend of vampires tells the
plight of one who is half-dead and half-alive, who looks into
the mirror and sees nothing. In darkness, a vampire must
charm and seduce victims in order to feed on them. Without
this supply, the vampire would cease to exist.

Every narcissist is desperate for a supply as well. (Kernberg,
1975) A person suffering from narcissistic wounds has little, if

any, identity. They need to see their reflection in people's faces and reactions to know they exist. A narcissist is like a symbiotic animal who must have a host: a person or group of people who can provide perfect, unconditional admiration and can focus on the narcissist's needs, to the exclusion of their own. This is the narcissist's "supply." If and when their primary source of validation is gone, the narcissist gropes desperately for another source of supply.

Narcissists get their identity from the love that others give to the *image* or false self they project. To narcissists, people are objects who exist only for their satisfaction. Since the narcissist uses other people's acknowledgment and attention to know that he or she exists, you can imagine how desperate this person is to maintain a perfect reflection. A narcissist focuses on potential sources of supply (people) and engulfs them with charm, concentrated attention, and contrived deep emotions.

It matters not whether this source even likes the narcissist! In the vampire legend, is it necessary for the victim to like the vampire in order to have their blood drained? No. Asking if a narcissist wants to be liked is like asking if it's important that your refrigerator likes you. Narcissistic supplies are objects, no more and no less.

A narcissistic client of mine named John called me late Friday afternoon just as I was about to go on a long weekend holiday. He said his live-in partner, Judy, had just broken up with him and that he couldn't cope. I mentioned that I was going to be out of the office over the weekend and that I would refer him to our staff psychiatrist whom John had previously met.

"Rokelle, you can't do that. You know how I need you. I'll destroy myself if you leave. I can't believe that going on your weekend vacation is worth that much to you. Where are your priorities?"

Since I'd been through this before with John, I knew that maintaining my boundaries was important and that my backing down inevitably increased John's narcissistic posturing. For that reason, I referred John to the staff psychiatrist. When I returned I found that John had been hospitalized for a day and a half, and I gave him a call.

"John, I understand that you were in the hospital and I wanted to check and see how you were doing today."

"Well, I'm kind of busy right now, but I'll tell you briefly that I'm doing really well!"

"How are you doing with the pain of losing your relationship?" I asked. "I hope you're feeling a little better about the breakup."

At that point in the conversation there was a long pause as if John had to recall who Judy was, because in the hospital he'd already attached himself to another patient named Susan!

If a narcissist must be liked in order to secure a supply, he does all he can to be liked. If he needs to be feared in order to be admired, he makes sure he is feared. A true narcissist doesn't really care what method he uses as long as he is being attended to. Attention—whether in the form of fame or infamy—is what it's all about. His world revolves around his constant mirroring. Dr. Sam Vaknin, and expert on NPD says, "Narcissists are like thermometers, and they react to human warmth, admiration, adoration, approval, applause, and attention as gradations of narcissistic temperature." (Vaknin, 2007)

Entrapping and maintaining a source of supply is more than a full-time job for the narcissist. The level of manipulation, seduction, and political shrewdness that it takes to cultivate and maintain a supply is honed to absolute perfection. This makes complete sense if you consider that his supply is as important to a narcissist as oxygen. It's a matter of emotional life or death. The problem is that there is never, ever enough.

If a narcissist's partner or coworker gives the correct responses, he or she will be held in high regard. The narcissist will go out of his way to please, cajole, and entertain. But for the individual who slips up, there's a price to pay. The narcissist will turn from Dr. Jekyll to Mr. Hyde, a raging maniac or a cold ice queen with no empathy. His or her mood swings can range from hopelessness to euphoria and are related to the quality or lack of narcissistic supply.

Think of a narcissistic supply as a gas tank with a very flexible hose. This feeding tank must be available all hours of the day and night when needed. A supply is the primary source for self-esteem, praise, nurturing, and attention until it's tapped completely dry. Eventually, when a supply is completely emptied, the narcissist will turn cold and start hunting for the next feeding tank.

FEEDING SOURCES

*"I used to be of the Hebrew persuasion,
but I converted to narcissism."*

—WOODY ALLEN, ACTOR, DIRECTOR

The top four sources of narcissistic supply are:

Spouse/partner
Children
Coworkers
Friends

If a narcissist begins to lose one of his sources of supply, he will respond with outrage or indignation. If the supply continues to diminish, he will become depressed, anxious, and angry—without remorse. True compassion and forgiveness are foreign to the narcissist; that is, unless he is giving a performance and simulating these emotions in order to maintain control.

A vulnerable child is one of the primary sources of supply for a narcissist. The kind of damage a narcissistic parent inflicts chokes the life out of a child's soul. One adolescent boy I encountered made this statement: "As a child, I used to be dazzled by my narcissistic parent's public demeanor. I wanted to take that person home with me or else live our entire family life in the protection of the public eye."

Several years ago I attended a world championship skating competition. There were thousands of spectators and I was able to get seats in the section where I could observe the talented skaters and their parents as well. At one point in the competition, a sixteen-year-old French skater was performing a difficult ice dance. Unfortunately this girl slipped, her score was lowered, and she was disqualified from the event.

Several minutes later this sad, teary teenage girl came up to the parents' section to be comforted, only to find her mom sitting with her arms folded and a scowl on her face. Nevertheless, this girl sat down next to her mother and put her head on her mother's shoulder. At this point the mother bolted up almost knocking her daughter off the bench and started scolding her in front of the rest of the crowd in the stands:

"What is the matter with you? Do you know how much we've sacrificed to get you this far? You've not only made a fool of yourself, but a fool of your family."

When this dejected girl got up to leave, her mother pulled her back down. For the duration of the competition, this teenager stayed by her mother's side. While other skaters were leaving to go out together, this girl knew where she had to be—or suffer the consequences.

As you can see by this example, it matters not whether a child has suffered, because to a narcissist, "It's all about me." The damage this causes to children is irreparable. As adults, these children will either pair with another narcissist, an alcoholic, or someone who demands full attention or admiration. Or, because of emotional starvation, they become narcissists themselves.

A narcissistic supply serves as both stage and audience. Narcissists will walk over you and use you. You may not see it at first because they need to entrap you. As a salesman, they need you to commit, to buy into their act. At first they are charming, flirtatious, attentive, and almost too perfect. Only afterwards will you discover their true nature. Unfortunately, this often occurs when you're so involved in the relationship that it's too late.

NARCISSISTIC RAGE: TREAD LIGHTLY AND DON'T MAKE WAVES

Controlling and manipulating their supply becomes a narcissist's modus operandi. If you've ever confronted a narcissist, you've no doubt witnessed why those who surround this person are afraid to disagree with or upset him. The intensity of narcissistic rage is frightening and vicious and derives from an infected, raw, and painful wound. What is particularly daunting to someone on the other side of this reaction is the seething, cold calculation that either accompanies narcissistic rage or replaces it. For example, narcissistic rage can manifest as a chilling hatred that is imbued with the qualities of power, invincibility, and calculation. This hatred underlies the desire for vengeance, for wanting to inflict pain and suffering, and for actually enjoying getting back at the person who failed the narcissist. (Almaas, 2004)

Narcissistic rage is provoked by the slightest insult—real or imagined—such as not being seen, understood, or appreciated in the way that one believes he is entitled to and deserves. What's so shocking is how this reaction can occur from seemingly small issues: dinner isn't ready yet; you didn't smile at him when he spoke to you; the checkbook was balanced incorrectly. In fact, you don't have to behave in any particular way to trigger narcissistic rage. A narcissist hates anyone who has (or seems to have) a rich inner life, more acclaim or success, more beauty, or more wealth. The pain this person feels will quickly transform into anger. It's difficult for anyone facing this rage to see that underlying this reaction is the envy and excruciating pain of not having what the other has, and the despair and shame that accompany the narcissist's belief that these things are unattainable.

NARCISSISTIC REMORSE: A PERFORMANCE

"I'm sorry that you irritate me."

—AN APOLOGY TO A COWORKER FROM A NARCISSISTIC MANAGER

No matter what the circumstances, narcissists will not define their behavior as abusive. Even when their reactions are explosive or violent, they justify their hurtful behavior by using words like "I'm helping," "I care," or "It is my responsibility to show you." Not only do they disguise their behavior as altruism, they cleverly shift the blame for any mistreatment to someone else.

Showing sincere remorse and being a narcissist are gross contradictions in terms. When a pathological narcissist offers forgiveness, it's often an insincere statement made from a position of authority. The motivation behind any contrition or form of regret is usually a well thought out manipulative ploy that's designed to achieve a particular goal. In the workplace or at home, if a narcissist feels in danger of losing his supply, or if he wants to achieve some goal, showing remorse comes in handy.

Narcissists do not register empathy; they lack the ability to put themselves in other people's shoes. When the rare apology is uttered, many partners or spouses become duped into thinking that "At last, he really understands how I've been treated." The harsh reality is that a narcissist acts empathetic only to draw in his prey. Although those involved in a relationship with a narcissist long to hear an apology, it is a futile and exhausting exercise to attempt. Trying to extract an apology from a narcissist never ends well.

In retaliation, the narcissist will resort to punishing their supply by physical or emotional abuse. Neglect and withholding love, attention, or money are also common recourses for the narcissist.

Bonnie was the head sales rep for a designer line of shoes. She was successful at her job and her sales record was far above her peers. She knew how to get the best out of her sales force through manipulation and threats, and her superiors loved the results. She could be extremely controlling and verbally abusive when she didn't get the results she wanted. She felt no remorse for her actions, but when Bonnie overstepped her bounds, she became obsequious and contrite. She knew that acting as if she'd done wrong could get much more out of her employees than any other technique. She'd send flowers, take them out for dinner, and make amends in any way she could. Her employees distrusted her, but the fear of Bonnie's wrath and the potential of her favor kept them in a perpetual cycle of abuse.

Narcissists are adept at manipulating their environment to achieve their primary goal: the survival of their false, grandiose self-concept. Like a gigantic balloon that needs a constant supply of air to stay afloat, narcissists are desperate people who have no qualms about obliterating anyone who stands in the way of their supply. The price one pays for being in a personal or professional relationship with one so cunning is devastating.

THE IMPACT
OF NARCISSISM
ON PERSONAL AND
PROFESSIONAL
RELATIONSHIPS

7

*H*ow to Recognize
a Narcissist

A narcissist is more than someone who likes to be the center of attention. This man or woman is a master of manipulation and disguise. The only way that you can recognize a narcissist is by frequent contact with him or her and by trusting your internal reactions.

Continued contact with a narcissist, whether professional, personal, or intimate, induces a sense of fear, terror, and anxiety. The terror is about angering this person and enduring the rage and contempt that result.

In the company of a narcissist, a normally self-assured individual can find themselves timid and ashamed for no good reason. Narcissists elicit profound and primitive wrath and hostility from sane and stable people. (Ashmun, 2003)

Despite one's most valiant efforts, nothing ever seems to please a narcissistic lover, parent, or coworker. The one who continually tries to please is left with diminished energy, power, and identity.

Despite all this, a narcissist can be extremely compelling. Usually bright, witty, attractive, and charming, they are sometimes impossible to resist. They are often well dressed, and take special care of their grooming. In a sense, they are the perfect salesperson, because they are selling them-selves—or to be more precise, selling their image. They want you to buy it, to be impressed, and to be captivated. If they have money they spend it on everything that will impress you. Clothes, jewelry, cars, kids, the house—everything must be perfect. You must love it. You must be bowled over and captivated because they are watching your every reaction. Their true self, however, is forever hidden and is a complete mystery to you.

An arrogant narcissist will often assume a special haughty posture. They are more than just vain—they are perfect—because they are actors who are putting on a show constantly. They love people who love them. They love gangs, cliques, clubs—anyplace people can congregate around them.

Narcissists are very good at reading people, at gauging people's reactions to what they say and how they say it. The Dale Carnegie course on how to influence people and make friends would be wasted on them: they could *give* the course. However, the styles of narcissists vary, and the ways in which they secure their supplies are as different as the stars.

TYPES OF NARCISSISTS

People with narcissistic personality disorder (NPD) can present with a wide range of psychopathologies. The more general DSM-IV description is of a cold type characterized by being aloof and arrogant. There is the classic arrogant, aggres-sive, self-absorbed, nonempathic type, but there is also the shy, embarrassed, hypersensitive type. An understanding of the types of narcissism helps to distinguish overtly relational varieties of narcissists from the angry, more introverted sort of narcissists. The table below helps clarify the differences.

The shy narcissist can win you over with her timid, kind, helpful, and unassuming presence. This narcissist often abhors the limelight and prefers to bask in the glow of another's aura.

ARROGANT NARCISSIST VERSUS SHY NARCISSIST

	Arrogant/ Aggressive	Shy/Covert
Self-concept	Grandiosity; entitlement; pre-occupation with fantasy; pseudo self-sufficiency	Inferiority; fragility; relentless search for glory and power; deterioration with realistic setbacks
Interpersonal Relationships	Numerous but shallow relationships; intense need for admiration; scorn for others; lack of empathy and remorse; inability to participate in group activities; valuing of children or work colleagues over spouse	Inability to depend on others; envy of others' talents, possessions, and relationships; lack of regard for generational boundaries (for example, incest may be present in family); disregard for others' time; refusal to respond to communications (letters, phone calls, and so forth)

ARROGANT NARCISSIST VERSUS SHY NARCISSIST *(continued)*

	Arrogant/ Aggressive	Shy/Covert
Social Adaptation	Socially charming; often successful; consistent hard work done mainly to seek admiration (pseudo-sublimation); intense ambition; preoccupation with appearances	Aimlessness; shallow vocational commitment; dilettante-like attitude; multiple but superficial interests; chronic boredom; aesthetic taste often ill-informed and imitative
Ethics, Morals, Ideals	Performance of modesty; pretended contempt for money; unevenly moral; apparent enthusiasm for sociopolitical affairs; will use abuse when disappointed	Readiness to shift values to gain favor; pathological lying; materialistic lifestyle; delinquent tendencies; excessive ethnic and moral relativism; irreverence toward authority
Love and Sexuality	Marital instability; cold and greedy seductiveness; extramarital affairs and promiscuity; uninhibited sexual life	Inability to remain in a relationship; inability to view the romantic partner as a separate individual; inability to comprehend the incest taboo; occasional sexual perversions

ARROGANT NARCISSIST VERSUS SHY NARCISSIST *(continued)*

	Arrogant/ Aggressive	Shy/Covert
Cognitive Style	Knowledgeable; decisive and opinionated; often strikingly articulate; egocentric perception of reality; love of language; fondness for shortcuts to acquisition of knowledge	Knowledge limited to trivia; forgetful of details; impaired in the capacity for learning new skills; changes meanings of reality when facing a threat to self-esteem

(Akhtar, 1989)

The shy narcissist may be less aggressive and bullying, but don't be fooled. Her shallowness, envy, and inability to be genuinely and consistently intimate with others cause just as much pain and rejection in relationships. The shy narcissist shares the following features with the arrogant narcissist:

- Sense of superiority and uniqueness.
- Lack of sustained commitment to others.
- Impaired capacity for empathy.
- Strong feelings of envy.
  (Ronningstam, 1998)

Have you ever been in a relationship with someone who's "not home"? Such a man or woman can shift from a doting admirer to a cold, resentful, and uninterested bystander. This exemplifies the shy (closeted) narcissist. These narcissists live in their fantasies. Their desires for power and glory aren't expressed and acted upon, but dreamt about to an exaggerated extent. These narcissistic fantasies prevent the shy narcissist from being present in relationships, and he often appears aloof or uninterested in what is going on around him. Or he may put on a performance, acting devoted, flattering, and caring. These types of narcissists are adept at showing warmth, but not closeness. They hitch their tail to a rising star and bask in its aura—until the day comes when they can no longer maintain the illusion of their chosen one's specialness. When this occurs their admiration simply dissolves, and they move on to some new object of worship. (Hotchkiss, 2003)

Shy/closeted narcissists avoid challenging situations. In fact, instead of demanding special attention from others, they may actually curry favor from people whose accomplishments they envy, while secretly harboring strong feelings of resentment and contempt. They tend to devote a considerable amount of time to ruminating over the unfairness of how little their true worth is appreciated, and how others get the recognition for things that *they* deserve. (Cooper & Ronningstam, 1992)

CODEPENDENCY VERSUS CLOSET NARCISSISM

"Codependency" is a term used to describe a person who becomes dependent upon another for emotional and physical validation. The codependent tries to control a relationship without directly identifying and addressing their own needs and desires. This phenomenon certainly causes pain and anguish, but it's also important to recognize that caretaking can be a stunning way to manipulate and receive the admiration the codependent feels they deserve.

I need to emphasize that caring for a suffering person is not synonymous with pathology. Genuine empathy, care, and compassion are valuable assets. Also, those who label themselves as codependent are not necessarily narcissists. However, in my clinical experience, the driving force of many a codependent is not altruism. In many circumstances, their motivations are self-serving and may derive from a refusal or inability to tolerate the discomfort of others. For example, if such a person's spouse is unhappy, her assumption is that it's about her. This causes her such anxiety that she becomes desperate to alleviate his pain. Why? In large part so she can feel better. She makes the sadness go away by becoming a shape-shifter: she will become whatever he wants her to be so she can get rid of *her* uneasiness.

I believe that many who define themselves as codependent may benefit by taking a hard look at the underlying motivation behind their caretaking. Could it be that we've labeled many closeted narcissists as codependents? There is definitely some overlap here. Codependency could certainly describe a type of narcissistic behavior where one devotes his life to another and fawns over someone in order to get self-worth—while at the same time feeling resentful, bitter, and contemptuous.

This is the type of codependent who does not realize how angry he is and at whom he is angry. Targeting the appropriate person is risky and may trigger a loss of the supply of approval and self-esteem the narcissist needs. Unarticulated anger is often misdirected and expressed inappropriately. Anger may be experienced as resentment, as an aggressive blowup, or as passive-aggressive acting out. The cognitive and verbal skills of this closeted, codependent narcissist are no match for an arrogant, cerebral narcissist.

This codependent, shy narcissist lives in the fantasy of the mate that will rescue her, adore her, respect her, and give her the attention she deserves. In other words, she maintains her silent grandiosity and omnipotence through a connection to someone she can "pump up." She has little self-respect, feels inferior, and is unable to see what's going on in front of her because she's so busy living in delusion. Male or female, the narcissistic codependent complains, whines, and is forever finding solace in friends who tell her, "You are a saint. I don't know how you can stand it." She may wear her suffering like a badge of courage, but under that thin veneer is disdain, bitterness, and deep contempt. As this veneer begins to erode, these underlying emotions manifest in passive-aggressive behavior.

It's not uncommon to see an arrogant narcissistic addict in relationship with a shy, closeted narcissist. This pairing is a lethal combination. Their symbiotic relationship can turn destructive, abusive, and irreparable. Both the arrogant and the closeted narcissist have wounds that developed in childhood. However, whether arrogant or hypersensitive, narcissists cause pain and suffering to those around them.

CEREBRAL AND SOMATIC NARCISSISTS

There are two general types of narcissists that utilize different methods to obtain their supply of admiration and attention: cerebral narcissists and somatic narcissists.

Cerebral Narcissists

The cerebral narcissist is haughty and intelligent and behaves like a human computer. He uses intellect or knowledge (real or pretended) to secure adoration, adulation, and admiration. The body and its maintenance are a burden and a distraction. For example, this man or woman often prefers celibacy (even if he or she has a spouse) rather than mature, interactive, emotionally-laden sex. Cerebral narcissists will try to impress others and woo them by their erudite knowledge and command of the language. And their consummate use of language is employed not just to impress, but also to obliterate anyone who stands in their way.

Arrogance is the most obvious quality of this narcissist, and ruthless ambition is most apparent as they climb to the top. The cerebral narcissist is convinced that he or she is unique and should only associate with other special or high-status individuals. In fact, when they are accused of making mistakes, you can bet that their reaction will be explosive and malicious.

There is a profound lack of empathy for others, and contempt is shown for inferiors, who are barely recognized as human. Decisions are made without thought to the consequences for those affected. All that is important is the pursuit of career goals. When this narcissist experiences a loss of supply he will become verbally offensive, caustic, and emotionally abusive. His or her verbal acuity is such that no one stands a chance at combating an assault by a cerebral narcissist.

Although this description is hardly flattering, such a person can be charming and have qualities widely admired in our society. Intelligence, status, and power attract attention. There can be the appearance of a genuine sense of benevolence towards others—though mostly in manipulative and patronizing ways.

Somatic Narcissists

A somatic narcissist uses her body, looks, and sexuality to romance, charm, and seduce. She is seductive, provocative, and obsessive-compulsive when it comes to her body. The somatic narcissist looks good, but the assets are all external. The values of this narcissist are familiar: image, fashion, glamour, youth, and beauty. This form of narcissism is so much a part of our times that it's hardly commented on!

The beauty of the somatic narcissist is only skin deep; their inner world can be empty and bleak. The intensity and depth of their needs are frightening. Curiously, this can lead to both "throw-away" relationships and a dependent relationship with an intimate other. The somatic narcissist's emotional needs can also be smothering and controlling, leading to a growing relationship crisis and eventually a sudden ending— sometimes with desperate consequences.

It's usually easy for this narcissist to attract people. The problem is sustaining a long-term relationship, even though these narcissists are afraid to be seen without their trophy male or female on their arm.

Somatic narcissists have no qualms about sharing the vivid details of their sex life, their divorce, their therapy discussion, or their underwear selections. These men and women cannot (or will not) respond to the cues of discomfort around them as they continue to prattle on about themselves. They just assume someone is interested and each day is a new opportunity for nonstop "show and tell."

Somatic narcissists have a marked intolerance for any imperfection in their partner. Once imperfection is acknowledged, it means the end of the fantasy of perfection. All this adds to a growing instability in relationships and to their explosive conclusions. (Vaknin, 2007)

Somatic narcissists often look, or think they look, significantly younger than they are; a youthful appearance is the primary source feeding their false self. Some somatic narcissists will emphasize their pride in their youthful looks by either dressing in clothes that were popular in their golden youth or wearing the styles of people much younger then they. (Ashmun, 2004) Imagine the pressure of living with this self-absorbed narcissist, where a "bad hair day" might mean the demise of a relationship!

While cerebral narcissists may tend to end their relationships with cutting words or a long diatribe of reasons, somatic narcissists tend to end their relationships with a flurry of high drama, the likes of which can be seen in bad daytime television. (Vaknin, 2007) Because of their histrionic natures, these narcissists will make sure that their partners know how they've suffered in the relationship and, ironically, how they haven't received the compassion and empathy they deserve. Their own misery takes precedence, and they literally can't tolerate the emotions of anyone close to them.

LURING VICTIMS IN: THE MANY OTHER FACES OF NARCISSISM

Narcissists are shape-shifters. They can turn themselves into whatever you want to see—but only long enough to lure you in. While cerebrals and somatics are the two dominant types of narcissists, the following narcissistic subtypes use various, sometimes distinct, strategies to seduce their victims into compliance.

The Extraordinary Lover

The extraordinary lover is a believer in the ideology of romantic love. This narcissist is an expert on romancing and providing excitement and stimulation for others. Initially, he may appear to have a rich emotional life, full of feeling and perhaps selective empathy. He may also exhibit some self-disclosure that enhances intimacy and heightens sexual passion. But the veneer hiding his broken self is quite thin and surprisingly brittle. (Pressman & Pressman, 1994) There is usually an underlying theme of grandiosity in his behavior: "No one can love you like I can. You may be in pain, but my love is special. It's worth it."

Initially, the partner of the extraordinary lover is idealized, but inevitably this partner falls from grace, sometimes suddenly. At this point, the narcissist acts as if he has lost respect for his partner. Meanwhile, the partner attempts to deny the contradictory behavior of the narcissist by trying even harder to please. Eventually the partner recognizes an unwelcome reality: during the intensity of unique love, the fracture lines can be ignored—for a while. But eventually intense romance gives way to disappointment.

The extraordinary lover has a remarkable intolerance for imperfection in his partner. And acknowledging imperfections means the end of the dream and often the end of the relationship. Unfortunately, narcissists extricate themselves from relationships with either a disappearing act or violent explosions of rage.

> Stan, for example, was a "hopeless romantic." He described himself quite realistically as a genuine sort of guy who was always faithful. He could also be amazingly selfless in a relationship, always forgiving, and yet his romances were fleeting. Something would "snap" after the quiet dinners, the romantic walks, and the poetry he wrote. He bragged that he was a fantastic lover, able to give mutual highs that he described as ecstatic. But eventually, reality would intrude. He began to notice and then obsess about such things as a scar on his lover's back, or the way that her bite wasn't perfect, or her inability to keep up the house to his standards. This reality brought him out of the clouds and crashing down to earth. He felt an empty void and an anguish that was excruciating. To him, that meant he was wasting his precious time in the current relationship. This pain would not dissipate until the next time he fell in love.

There are at least two aspects to the extraordinary lover's vulnerability. The inner self is highly vulnerable to any slights—real or imagined—and bleeding wounds persist from past romantic encounters. Secondly, jealousy is a common denominator in this type of narcissistic bond, as it is in Sarah and Nick's relationship.

Nick decided to go to a movie with his friends. Sarah was working late that night, and he hadn't seen his buddies for weeks. They chose a movie that starred Angelina Jolie and all the guys loved it. When Nick came home, Sarah was waiting at the door and he knew she was in one of her moods. She grilled him about where they went, what time they got there, and what they talked about. She asked detailed questions about the movie. When Nick touted the acting abilities of Angelina Jolie, Sarah became tense and asked if she found this actress more appealing than she was. Before Nick had a chance to answer, Sarah stormed away, slammed the door, and refused to let him in the bedroom. Nick spent another evening on the couch by himself.

The Dictator

For the dictator, grandiosity is expressed outwardly in terms of success and possessions. There is never enough achievement or material objects to match the inner image of success. Others are often used in exploitive ways with a sense of entitlement: "Why shouldn't I do this? I deserve only the very best!"

Robert was a high achiever. He was the youngest, most competent senior executive in the history of a large computer company. The executive management team loved the results he produced, but the costs were less obvious. Gradually his reputation was tarnished with growing complaints and escalating numbers of employee resignations in his department. When the CEO called a meeting, Robert didn't seem to care. He knew his talent was worth the work of six "underlings" and that he was irreplaceable. Despite this grandiosity and the continued effect on other personnel, the president of the company kept him on the job because he couldn't afford to lose such a gifted executive.

Although the characteristics of the dictator are hardly flattering, such a person can be affable and have qualities widely admired in our society. Status and power are attractive (as noted earlier), and companies are often willing to put up with bad behavior in exchange for high profit margins. (Bursten, 1986)

Because the dictator needs to use power and control, he seems to require a different set of rules in relationships. A partner may experience this as feeling very possessed, highly restricted, and at times, abused. This narcissist cultivates the trophy relationship in which an attractive partner is displayed along with other tokens of status, and the relationship is usually filled with conflict. The dictator has an impoverished inner life with little to give in any emotional sense. The partner of this narcissist feels a growing dissatisfaction and emptiness. The demands of intimacy are overwhelming and even frightening for the dictator. This leads to perpetual pain and inner turmoil because the dictator doesn't understand how or why his or her partner can't appreciate their outstanding abilities and just shut up about all the rest. (Stevens, 1999)

The Raging Bull

A barely controlled rage simmers below the surface of many narcissists and often strikes at anyone nearby. Unhappiness is expressed with increasing hostility. There are episodes of explosive rage triggered by irrational, mystifying, unexplainable causes.

What's most characteristic of this type of narcissist is hypersensitivity to any perceived insult—intended or not. Everything is taken personally and usually interpreted as an attack. What sparks the rage is narcissistic injury. The world may be seen in only black-and-white terms. Projecting blame is a knee-jerk reaction. The subjective experience of rage may be accompanied by interpretations of spiteful intent and may have a paranoid quality.

Betty, for example, ruled her family with her unpredictable explosions of anger for years. Gradually she alienated everyone. After sixteen years of marriage, her husband, Eric, left her for a younger woman. It was his "bid for a new life," but he then instituted a custody fight for the three teenage children. Perhaps surprising to no one but Betty, the children expressed a unanimous desire to live with their father.

A relationship with someone like Betty is always unpredictable. But this isn't the whole story. Some raging bulls can be very loving and generous in affection. The aftermath of hideous conflict can be intense, sexual encounters that feel even more erotic because of the earlier menace. Some partners actually develop a traumatic bond to this type of behavior and find it impossible to leave. Raging bulls can be extremely controlling and it's almost the norm that the relationship will be abusive.

Anger can be a healthy emotion; however, it's not a primary emotion. In other words, it's important to focus on the underlying, perhaps more uncomfortable, feelings the raging bull experiences. These may include sadness, fear, shame, or grief. All narcissists lack the capacity to handle intense emotions including, but not limited to, anger.

The Con Artist

The con artist is charming and extremely persuasive, engaging, smooth, and inviting. Unfortunately, these qualities are too often a facade for a very disturbed personality. Behind the "you can trust me" messages, you will find a malicious goal. Sabotaging a business partner or even cheating someone out of a pension check is not beyond the realm of a con artist.

> Susan came into the attorney's office sobbing uncontrollably. Frank, her partner of six months, had gone on a business trip for what she thought would be a brief six days. The evening before he left, he asked her if he could borrow her car, since his was out of commission. She was puzzled when he didn't call her at work to say good-bye. When she returned to her apartment that evening she discovered, to her horror, that he had loaded up her car with her precious belongings and fled. She found a note that said that she owed him for his putting up with her these last few months.

The con artist is brutal in relationships. He delights in fooling the susceptible lover with betrayals such as sexual infidelity, fraud, or criminal conspiracy until trust is completely obliterated. This type of narcissist relishes intrigue and derives considerable joy in planning deception. Conniving and manipulation are always at the core of his strategy.

The damage inflicted is deepened as this narcissist treats the victim with contempt, and he feels absolutely justified because this individual was so easily fooled and therefore deserved this treatment. The cruelty of the con artist's game and impact on his victim is always devastating. Yet this type of narcissist believes it's always the fault of the mate: "If it weren't for her, I wouldn't be driven to have affairs," is a common cry. It can be likened to psychic vandalism. The resulting damage is not easily repaired and may take a lifetime of rebuilding boundaries. Trusting someone again may seem highly unlikely.

The con artist comes in many disguises and is difficult to identify until a partner or coworker has been duped emotionally, physically, or financially. The narcissistic quality in the con artist is very dark and can appear more akin to an antisocial or even psychopathic personality. The difference is that a narcissist primarily reserves his punishment for those with whom he has a relationship.

The Illusion Seeker

The illusion seeker has an elaborate inner world. For this narcissist, the only joy and excitement that exists is in the world of fantasy. The real world intrudes, naturally, but it is exactly that—an intrusion and often resented. He or she may have an external appearance of superficiality, flightiness, and emptiness. There may also be considerable social anxiety and awkwardness—that is, inner riches, outer poverty.

The primary commitment of this narcissist is always to his or her inner world. The external impression given may not be of a self-centered person, but within there is always a hero present in some guise or other. Only in the fantasy is this individual significant, beautiful, admired, loved, and everything wonderful.

Reality is cold and harsh and to be avoided as long as possible. There is a pervasive distrust of outer reality that is often frustrating and withholding. The illusion seeker's needs can be so powerful that retreat from the world is necessary. Rather than enhancing personal growth, fantasy feeds the illusion of independence. It is the perfect escape for the perfectionist.

Derek was a young man who spent his evenings playing video games. It was through these games that he played out his fantasies of acquired magical powers. He had a couple of friends, but friendship was based only on involvement in these games. As he grew, his illusions of power, control, and magical ability were immediately available in his fantasy life. With this illusion in tact, why should he have to endure the imperfections of others? He was far above their domain and let them know it. If anyone insisted that Derek conform, he would behave indignantly. When he eventually found a girlfriend, he learned how to manipulate her as skillfully as he manipulated the players in his fantasy game.

Although it's easier to be an illusion seeker in isolation, a narcissist needs a relationship; therefore, a mate needs to be someone who buys into the fantasy of grandeur. The problem is that an illusion-seeking partner, spouse, or mate will eventually become disillusioned. Their loyalty is not to the present, but to their inner world, which no one else can enter and which provides immediate gratification. The way back to reality is to shift the loyalty from the realm of fantasy to the world everyone else shares.

The Sufferer

You mean a sufferer can be narcissistic? Absolutely! For the sufferer, anguish is usually the only focus, the only awareness that makes them unique. Personal identity is constructed around being in pain, or being a victim, or being a survivor. Pain justifies a pervasive self-focus, with parasitic demands and exploitive relationships. (Vaknin, 2007)

A sufferer often carries around a lot of emotional baggage, but letting go of the past is not an option. Without this history, the sufferer would lose his or her grounding for self-pity. In fact, the art of self-pity is perfected and provides an endless source of raw material.

Naturally, this pain is not ordinary pain. The narcissistic pain of the sufferer is laced with self-important features. "No one has suffered as I have suffered" is this narcissist's only consolation. There may even be a transcendent dimension with religious meaning to this suffering: God sanctions the pain.

Joanna exaggerated her mild physical problems to anyone who would listen. Time after time, every medical test came back within normal range, and the doctors determined that she was basically healthy. Convinced that she could not be normal, Joanna turned to the New Age movement. When she didn't get enough attention from this community, she went to the church. She came to the conclusion that she was divinely sanctioned, a vocation to suffer alone, but not in silence.

The sufferer most easily forms relationships with someone

who "needs to be needed," most often a rescuer. The victim story can be captivating and even controlling. It is a way of exercising considerable power in a relationship or family. But the inevitable lack of balance can backfire and this narcissist begins to treat their support with thinly veiled contempt. It is hardly surprising that friends and family eventually feel manipulated and resentful. When everyone leaves, the sufferer has yet another reason for self-pity.

It is important to make a distinction between healthy and unhealthy pain. What needs to be faced may be painful, but this is the way of growth. In contrast, avoiding necessary pain leads to what's been called "dirty pain." The sufferer is a master at this kind of endless self-defeating misery. This is the narcissist's defense against experiencing legitimate pain while at the same time getting the attention they feel they deserve.

The Rescuer

The rescuing narcissist is usually seen as virtuous. Such people seem to inhabit the high moral ground of business or social causes. They are usually helpful, considerate, and nice to those whom they're trying to save—until someone gets in the way. Rescuers see themselves as saviors, redeemers, and liberators and have absolutely no tolerance for insignificant relationships like children or family.

Carl was working in a free legal service in an impoverished inner city area. He had an unusual fanaticism for his work. But as a fanatic he could be scathing of other members of the legal profession who were not as motivated by his high ideals. In fact, he'd spend his spare time lecturing other members of his profession as if he was an orator and they were the ignorant and sinful. He often worked eighty-hour weeks and would take calls late into the night. He found it impossible to go on vacations since he believed, "My people need me." Ironically, he treated his family as if they didn't exist and was impatient, withdrawn, and quite cold with his children and spouse.

Why is this narcissistic? After all, aren't some people just being helpful? Behind the rescuer's helpfulness, however, is veiled grandiosity and a false sense of empowerment: "I'm the only one that can really change things, so don't get in my way!" The rescuer has little tolerance for anger, anxiety, fear, or sadness. His goal, ultimately, is to control others in order to keep his own guts quiet! The common ground of rescuers is remaining in control, being emotionally intrusive, and not acknowledging needs. The rescuer may hide in helping professions, including psychology, social work, medicine, pastoral care, and counseling. The blurred boundaries that ensue in these professions are part of a narcissistic pattern that have hideous consequences—especially for those that entrust their physical, emotional, or spiritual care to these people. Some of the worst boundary violations are made by those to whom we entrust our emotional and spiritual well-being, The role of the rescuer is most heinous when there is a guru or messianic quality in a religious leader, physician, or therapist.

Although each of these types is something of a caricature, looking at their prime characteristics illuminates the complex therapeutic and relational issues they present. It is imperative to understand that these people are in torment and that narcissism is in part a defense. As analyst Neville Symington (Symington, 2002) observed, "When narcissism is opted for, it is to protect the individual against appalling pain."

Dealing with the Narcissist in the Workplace

"Mr. Harris, you're always late.
Why don't you wear a watch?"
"Because nothing starts until I get there anyway?"

Workplace narcissists are common. You can usually tell who they are because they think they should be running the show and consider their coworkers to be lowly underlings. They make no attempt to hide their grandiosity and contempt for others. Working with such a person is demeaning and stressful. He or she is adept at twisting knives, cutting people up, humiliating them, and frightening them, making them feel insecure about their jobs.

Supervising someone with narcissism is nearly impossible. The exception to this is if this employee wants to manipulate the boss for admiration or attention. Then, you'll find him or her effusive, charming, and eager to please. A supervisor in this situation won't be able to understand the complaints they're receiving from other employees who can't tolerate the narcissist's behavior. The following is a story of one such employee who was detested by his co-workers.

Ron acts superior to everyone at work. He talks to others in a disdainful tone of voice and always has a sarcastic comment. He's known as the Dalai Ron among his peers and no one can stand to be with him. The truth is that Ron is insecure and only derives a sense of self from other people's impressions of him. He needs his self-esteem to be propped up by others in order to feel any sense of worth. If Ron weren't such an outstanding real estate broker, his behavior wouldn't be tolerated at work. He can't endure any form of criticism, and his supervisor has resorted to giving Ron feedback by e-mail. Ron caused such havoc in his agency that he was given an office that separated him from the rest of the staff. Of course, this just fed his arrogant behavior and added to the resentment of the staff.

People tend to put up with narcissists at work because they're usually industrious. No matter how badly they behave, they seem to be able to stay gainfully employed. Usually, this is because workplace narcissists are likely to be ingratiating to their superiors. Therefore, their negative characteristics may not be as apparent to those above them as to those at their level or below. Furthermore, narcissists are likely to treat superiors with deference because they can provide them with a primary supply of grandiosity and power.

Narcissists have such drive to prove how superior they are that they often acquire positions of real power or public notoriety. They are the sort of people who, given the right circumstances, can doggedly work their way to the top, regardless of what they have to do to get there. On the surface, it seems that they have a glorious image of themselves and a manifest destiny. Their lack of empathy for others can be a positive asset when it comes to making tough business or political decisions.

The following is a list of some of the people who've shaped our lives partly because of their narcissistic traits, according to Michael Maccoby, author of *The Productive Narcissist* (Maccoby, 2003): Bill Gates, Napoleon Bonaparte, Leonardo da Vinci, Abraham Lincoln, Richard Nixon, Coco Channel, Orson Welles, Marlon Brando, Marcel Proust, James Joyce, Vincent Van Gogh, Henry Ford . . . and the list goes on.

Can narcissism be a positive characteristic? Possibly, when it comes to achieving big things, but not in creating a productive work environment. The problem for narcissists is that, eventually, the trail of human damage they leave in their wake tends to catch up with them. So do the fantasies they weave to prop up their glorious images of themselves. The political psychologist Betty Glad points out that once rulers have established positions of power the reality-testing capabilities diminish. (Glad, 2004) Often the narcissistic fantasies that have been held in check until they gain power are likely to become guides for action once they have achieved it, and the inevitable result is downfall.

WHY WOULD YOU HIRE A NARCISSIST?
"Show Me the Money!"

Popular books are written that give specific directions on how to cultivate narcissistic behavior. Robert Greene, author of *The 48 Laws of Power, The Art of Seduction,* and *The 33 Strategies of War,* calls these books "How to Be a Jerk" manuals. (Greene, 2000, 2003, 2007) Greene says that shy individuals trying to succeed in social and professional situations may often purchase these books, but it's clear that many others covet the qualities of power, control, and manipulation. In fact, he reports on an interesting letter he received from an inmate at Rikers Island prison who used his books to take over Cell Block B.

The business world actually encourages narcissism in its leaders. Why? Because in order to maintain the stature they long for, narcissists are driven and often quite willing to make personal sacrifices in order to succeed. In fact, pretentious narcissists can be beneficial in terms of the effort and perseverance they exhibit at work.

In today's work culture, there are clear benefits in hiring a narcissist. Narcissists have little problem making tough decisions without being distracted by empathy, sadness, or guilt. You won't find this type of employee obsessing about how their actions affect co-workers, unless it causes them to lose power. Their vigilance in maintaining their supply of admiration motivates them to seek out and pay attention to the feedback of superiors, clients, and customers. As a result, narcissists are cunning in order to avoid the terror of personal failure. Their actions are often well thought out and they're able to scrupulously assess the risks and rewards of any decision.

This type of employee is practiced at being charismatic and skilled. These attributes, combined with grandiose, albeit delusional, visions can attract followers and actually inspire loyalty and dedication. In the public or private sector, business owners find that some employees can be motivated and even feel rewarded by even a slight amount of attention or regard from a powerful narcissist. A narcissist in the workplace is highly motivated both by self-esteem and by social esteem. His or her presence may create a very dysfunctional and stressful work environment, but from a financial standpoint, it makes sense to many companies to hang on to this employee.

Despite the so-called advantages of employing narcissists,

the problems that he or she causes in the workplace may not be worth the extreme effort it takes to maintain this employee. For one thing, even though narcissists may have visionary goals, they can just as easily ignore or deny reality in order to have their needs met. This can lead to huge mistakes, miscalculations, and catastrophe. Further, a narcissist can exploit the organization in order to attain these goals. In these cases, success can lead to failure if this employee accumulates too much power and prestige to the point where a supervisor loses control.

David dressed to kill, always had a smile on his face, and had a dynamic way of speaking. When he first arrived at the company, other employees were drawn to him and even shared their strategies in working the stock market. Dave proved himself skilled with clients and slowly developed recognition by his superiors. He knew exactly how to move to the top and became romantically involved with his boss, Cynthia. During intimate moments, he'd share his visions with her regarding how he could move the business into the Fortune 500 bracket. He knew of a company that was about to go public in the area of a new, anti-aging drug. Cynthia was at first doubtful, but gradually was swept away by David's confidence. The other brokers were leery, and a few quit. However, many were persuaded that "this guy knew what he was doing." Under David's direction, the corporation invested over half of its assets into this unknown enterprise. When the Federal Drug Administration kept postponing its approval of the new drug, David's corporation was forced to borrow money and eventually the business landed in bankruptcy.

Although a narcissist can make difficult decisions without being overly prejudiced by other's reactions, this employee is powerfully influenced by mood fluctuations. For example, if a narcissistic woman doesn't get the appreciation she feels she deserves by someone in the office, the effect could be disastrous. She may cancel projects involving this coworker; she may even start the process of having this person removed from the staff. In other words, it's entirely possible for this woman to make vital choices for the wrong reasons. And even though narcissists can be risk-takers, grandiosity can lead to too much risk, while fear of failure can result in too little.

Have you ever tried to give feedback to a narcissist? Or have you ever been supervised by a narcissist and tried to *get* helpful feedback? Narcissists don't generally seek out feedback unless they're sure it's going to be stellar. It's also likely that they're not going to accept feedback unless it's praise. If you try to get this person to listen to an accurate account of their performance, you may witness rage, tantrums, or the kind of manipulation that makes a magician look like an amateur. Since workplace narcissists tend to surround themselves with loyal and uncritical staff, it's highly likely that mistakes will either go unnoticed or unspoken.

Although narcissists can inspire others to make sacrifices, they're unlikely to empathize enough with fellow employees to know what truly motivates them. And in terms of the future of an organization, narcissists may not pick or groom a successor. If they do, it will likely be someone who is able to curry favor with or give adequate attention to the narcissist, not necessarily someone who is capable.

If a person with these tendencies is supervising you, it's doubtful that you're going to receive the mentoring or coaching needed to succeed in your job. And if you question or disagree with the feedback a narcissist gives you, it's probable that you'll be out of favor and that your work life will be made miserable. Giving appreciation to subordinates who take initiative isn't likely to happen where a narcissist is concerned. Instead, you may be exploited and overworked with little consideration for personal cost. And it's highly unlikely that you'll be granted a "voice" to offer suggestions or to air grievances.

If you ingratiate yourself and don't disagree, if you do whatever is asked of you without question or hesitation, you'll be held in high regard by the workplace narcissist. You will be considered a source of supply, a stepping-stone that can lead the narcissist to greater and loftier goals. After all, your needs and your coworkers needs are trivial compared to your narcissistic supervisor's desire to achieve his or her grand destiny.

To say that a narcissist isn't a team player is another gross understatement. Workplace narcissists have an inherent reluctance to share credit or take blame, which can be an eternal source of frustration for team members. The conflicts that result from those who deliberately or inadvertently threaten their esteem resemble the kind of craziness that erupts in dysfunctional families. It may feel like vicious sibling rivalry or vindictive parental abuse.

No wonder turnover is higher for those reporting to narcissistic managers. (Dattner, 2003) Groups that are supervised by narcissistic managers can be split along the lines of who the manager does or doesn't favor. This is when stress-related absences and low productivity and morale can destroy the work environment and erode the organization's core values and purpose.

Do the costs outweigh the advantages of employing narcissists? Not necessarily, if they can be skillfully reigned in by managers who have the capability to do so and aren't afraid to confront what they see.

SURVIVAL SKILLS FOR WORKING
WITH A NARCISSIST

Setting limits with a workplace narcissist can feel like tossing a boomerang and watching helplessly while it comes back and smashes you in the head. However, it's possible to use your knowledge of a narcissist to your advantage. There are ways to set boundaries that allow you to massage their fragile egos and still maintain your dignity.

The most important aspect in speaking with narcissistic colleagues or bosses at work is mindfulness and preparation. If you want to commit emotional suicide, then walk into a narcissist's office and wing it, especially if you have something critical that needs to be said.

The next time you have to confront a narcissist, remember the three ingredients of empowerment:

- **Presence:** How do you want to show up in the room? Do you want to convey insecurity and doubt or confidence and charisma?
- **Communication:** Be clear about what you want to say. Practice your approach so that you don't have to stumble over your words.
- **Timing:** Wait for the right time to get across your message.
  (Owens, 1999)

Before you deliver a message to a narcissist, take the time to summon your energy and vitality. Think about what nonverbal impression you want to make. How you show up in the room gives a narcissist the first clue as to whether you will be dismissed, eaten for lunch, or worth the time to be listened to. Avoid projecting an awful outcome to your encounter. Instead, focus on the kind of outcome you'd like and how it will feel when it's accomplished. Self-sabotage comes from allowing your anxiety to get the best of you.

An organization can devise strategies to maximize the benefits and minimize the risks of narcissism in its ranks. The following suggestions will prevent a business from becoming a chaotic and highly dysfunctional system:

Ten Suggestions for Minimizing the Impact of Narcissistic Employees:

1. Be mindful about the potential consequences of recruiting, hiring, and promoting narcissistic managers.
2. Consider the impact of narcissism on the culture of the workplace.
3. Surround the narcissist with capable and confident advisors who are willing to disagree.
4. Carefully monitor the risks that the narcissist is taking.
5. Track the employee turnover statistics for narcissistic managers.
6. Provide incentives for managers to retain staff and to coach, mentor, and cultivate successors.
7. Find indirect or nonthreatening ways to give feedback to narcissists. (This may include using humor or giving feedback in writing.)
8. Scrutinize the incentives that the narcissist offers to lower level staff.
9. Reward the group rather than providing individual incentives.
10. Consider carefully what role a narcissist should play on a team.

If you're working for a narcissist you may have to give a performance to survive, and this may not be worth the exertion and the toll it takes on personal integrity. Dr. Sam Vaknin, author of *Malignant Self Love,* (Vaknin, 2007) has some suggestions for those who must retain their jobs and need to preserve their sanity:

- The best way to cope with a narcissist at work is to avoid them. When you can't, try your best to limit your involvement and surround yourself with supportive people who are capable of healthier interactions. (Hotchkiss, 2003)
- Never disagree with the narcissist or contradict him or her publicly.
- Never offer him or her friendship. You will be used.
- Look awed by whatever attribute matters to them (for instance, their professional achievements, good looks, or success with men).
- Never remind them of life outside their bubble, but if you do, connect it somehow to their sense of grandiosity.
- Avoid comments that might directly or indirectly impinge on self-image, omnipotence, judgment, omniscience, skills, capabilities, professional record, or even omnipresence.
- Avoid the inclination to apologize. If apologies are appropriate, you can always do so later. Apologizing to a narcissist only fuels the fire and reinforces the notion that you are a victim.
- Avoid sentences that start with:
  "I think you overlooked . . . made a mistake. . . should have known . . ."
  "You don't know . . ."
  "Did you know . . ."
  "You weren't here yesterday so we . . ."
  "You can't (or) you really should . . ."

A narcissist perceives statements like those above as rude impositions and they will no doubt cause irritation or even an outburst. The workplace narcissist will also be put on the defensive, and the retribution that ensues may not be worth the price. Are these suggestions manipulative? Absolutely. Unfortunately they are the tactics needed to survive working closely with a narcissist.

HANDLING NARCISSISTIC BULLIES, CRITICS, AND BRAGGERS AT WORK

Bullies

When we're bullied, we often do one of two things: counter-attack or acquiesce. Neither serves to shift the bullying dynamic. With a narcissistic bully, try to remain cordial and professional. You don't necessarily have to be friendly, but it's in your own best interest to maintain a businesslike demeanor. In order to do this, however, it's imperative to set boundaries. For example, if someone bullies you and charges into your office and talks down to you, it would be appropriate to say, "Hold on a minute here. I am happy to talk to you about this, but I'm not going to talk about it in this way." Respectfully letting a bully know that you have boundaries won't necessarily change the behavior, but you've put the person on notice that you won't tolerate this kind of intrusion, and you've maintained your self-respect. The challenge is to maintain your self-control, contain your reactions, and keep from shrinking in the face of bullying. (See page 192.)

Lois Frankel, an executive business coach, advises that initially it's not a good idea to turn to human resources for help.

"When you turn to HR for help, you wind up looking as if you don't know how to handle conflicts in the workplace. That's not good for your career or your reputation." (Frankel, 2004) There may come a time, however, when the abuse becomes so intolerable that you'll have to report a narcissist and get assistance. Chances are quite high that you're not the only one who's complained. Certainly, if this person is sexually inappropriate or physically abusive, then it needs to be addressed immediately. In the case of bullies, however, I would advise that you turn to HR only after other strategies have failed.

Critics

Narcissists can be brutal with their criticism. The harsh criticism from a narcissist usually doesn't have much to do with the reality of a given situation, but with the narcissist's feelings of not being admired, being a personal failure, or experiencing shame triggered by the situation. The secret to dealing with this type of behavior is to resist taking the bait. Acknowledge the narcissist and even thank him for the feedback. That's it—full stop. And remember that just because the narcissist criticizes doesn't mean that what he's saying is the truth. With all feedback, of course, you must weigh the information and see if there is a kernel of reality in what is said; but that doesn't mean that you must take it all in.

Don't let the issue of the criticism escalate into a battle. Avoid getting into an argument or power struggle around the issue because you will lose. If the critic is the boss or a supervisor, you need to show that you're listening, but if his behavior persists you will gradually learn to blow it off.

If you're being criticized in a meeting or another public place, I'd suggest you look the narcissist in the eye, nod your head as if you're listening, and say that you'll think about what he's saying and get back to him. This is another area where boundaries need to be set. You might say, "I really do value your feedback, but I think this is a conversation that should take place at another time." If you're in a meeting and feel as if you've been embarrassed and you don't want to have a meltdown or seem submissive, you can say, "Let me think about that." Then later, after the meeting, you can say, "I didn't have a problem with your feedback. I had a problem with the manner in which it was delivered. Here's what would work better in the future." (See page 200 for workplace and boundaries.)

What if I Can't Leave My Job?

Having activities and people outside of work that are important to you help you maintain perspective. If you're in a job where you can't tolerate the dynamics of narcissistic managers or coworkers but have to stay there for financial reasons, it is crucial for you to find some area of your life that brings you joy, relief, and serenity. Clinging to your passion and your purpose in life and in work is critical. Narcissists have the ability to mesmerize us. We may become so anxious about pleasing them and not incurring their wrath that we lose our bearing and our dignity. Our priorities may become skewed and our work life may bleed over all aspects of our existence.

Although financial pressures for many are acute, in the last analysis those who give up what's important to them to meet the needs of a job often don't have anything to go home to. Or they don't want to deal with what they have to go home to. Many who choose this path in their work life do so unconsciously. But inevitably this becomes an empty and lonely existence. To face what's going on in our lives is the first step on the journey to well-being and peace.

Narcissists and Intimacy: A Contradiction in Terms

"I was married to a narcissist for sixteen years.
It's the closest thing there is to hell on earth."

—ANONYMOUS

hen it comes to relationships, the narcissist's dilemma lies in the paradox of intimacy. The narcissist is torn between his desperate need to obtain admiration and attention—and his fervent wish to be left alone. This wish springs both from contempt and feelings of superiority. An intimate relationship means allowing one's sense of self to be merged with another's. For a narcissist, this presents the danger of losing oneself altogether. (Solomon, 1992)

The narcissist is filled with internal conflict. For example, narcissists have little self-awareness and yet are hyperaware of people's reaction to them. They struggle between dependency and contempt, neediness and devaluation, seeking and avoiding, turning on the charm to attract adoration and being overcome by irate reactions to the most minuscule annoyances. These conflicts lead to rapid cycling between gregariousness, seclusion, anxiety, and rage. The narcissist's search for adulation and admiration is a futile attempt to restore a sense of connection, and there is an illusion of safety and control in being highly esteemed by others. For a narcissist, the need to feel special replaces their desire for connection.

A person with narcissistic wounds enters a relationship with the expectation that the significant other will understand what they need at all times. While we all enter intimacy with the hope that our beloved will attend to our emotions, a person with narcissistic wounds demands that his partner attend to the emotions that he cannot tolerate in himself.

Sole attention and admiration is what we should have received as babies from parents who loved us. Perhaps it's what we dream of in romantic relationships. As we mature, however, we learn that this is an unrealistic expectation and is probably not going to happen on any regular basis. Sadly, narcissists never reach this level of maturity and live in a perpetual cycle of disappointment, hurt, and anger.

My narcissistic husband (who I'm finally divorcing after 18 years) said, on our very first date: "You'll never do better than me." One of many warning statements that I ignored; his persuasive charm won out. A charm that disappeared, literally, days after we were married. One incident occurred three weeks after our wedding, when he was in a towering rage after returning from a trip. I was completely perplexed at what was angering him. When I finally asked him, he turned to me with the most spiteful glare, and said: "*You!* You are what is wrong with me. You are always irritating me." But there was no action or incident related to me that he could recount. In fact, he had been away at a trade show while I was deliberately asked to stay home. For years, I racked my brain to figure out what I'd done to cause his malicious outbursts. Nothing was ever good enough.

It doesn't take long for a narcissist to become bored and start searching for greener pastures. Dominance and control become an essential strategy in narcissistic relationships and very soon the vitality is drained from the connection. This contributes to the narcissist's inevitable boredom and the quest for newness and excitement. It's not unusual to see a once-loving partner quickly morph into a man or woman with a roving eye, seductive encounters with coworkers or clerks, and clandestine pornographic interests.

Welcome to My World— Where There Is No "You"

It isn't possible to have a real, meaningful emotional relationship with a narcissist, until his defense mechanisms are discarded through years of intensive therapy. But that fact certainly doesn't stop some of us from trying. If this has happened to you, please be gentle with yourself. Keep in mind that there is nothing quite like being courted by a narcissist. When he or she is trying to win you over, there is no one who can deliver the kind of mesmerizing attention that makes you feel completely loved and cared for. Narcissists are some of the most compelling, bright, and charming people on the face of the earth! They will use these qualities purposefully to get what they need from you and other family members. After a time, however, their wounds will surface and you'll wonder what happened to the person who courted you—then disappeared after the courtship:

Judy was swept off her feet. She'd never been romanced this way before. She'd noticed Jason at the office party, and who wouldn't! He was the center of attention and had the charisma and charm that made him the fantasy of many women in the office. When Jason finally asked her out, she was elated beyond words. Judy was mesmerized by his intelligence, his commanding presence, and his romantic nature. They would talk until the wee hours of the morning, and when he finally proposed several months later, she was the envy of many in her office. That is, until Judy confided to a coworker that during the honeymoon, Jason was cold and uninterested. Apparently, the first evening in Hawaii, Judy suggested that Jason change his tie for dinner because it had a spot on it. Jason responded with fury and then gave her the silent treatment the rest of the trip. Judy quietly cried herself to sleep for two nights, wondering what she'd done to offend him so terribly. Despite her crying, Jason paid no attention and it wasn't until Judy apologized that he slowly began to display the charm that Judy remembered. To avoid offending Jason in the future, she vowed never to voice her opinion, even when it was asked for.

For spouses or partners of narcissists, it's crucial to remember that they will spin your reality to make theirs less painful.

One of the most common defense mechanism they use is projection. In projection, they transfer to you a characteristic of themselves that they find too painful to accept. In other words, what a narcissist denies and is too terrified to face he will attribute to you. Then, through manipulation and mind games, he will proceed to mold you to conform to his prejudices. After a while it becomes hard to distinguish what is real from what is being projected. We begin to doubt our reality and question whether we're the crazy ones and our disordered significant others (SOs) are right about what they say.

Nothing is more hated by a narcissist than an expression of intimacy like, "I love you." It provokes severe reactions and bitter rage. At times a narcissist may use this expression to lure a potential supply. When expressed by another, however, it is detestable. Narcissists identify being loved with being possessed, engulfed, and inevitably discarded. Loving someone also involves knowing a person intimately, and a true narcissist believes that they are "above knowing." A response of "I love you" drags this person down to a raw form of human vulnerability, which is absolutely intolerable.

From the perspective of a narcissist, a person who claims to love them is a fraud, a liar, or blind. "After all," as one narcissistic client told me in a vulnerable moment, "There's nothing whatsoever to love about me, so how can I ever trust him again!" Since the narcissist can't stand the fact that she may have chosen an idiot or an impostor for a mate, a statement of genuine caring is also an indirect slam against her judgment.

Tragically, many enter into relationships with narcissists hoping that pouring their love, compassion, and support onto their beloved will heal the pain their partners feel. This is a damaging belief when you're entering into a relationship with anyone; in a relationship with a narcissist, it's perilous. This assumption will drain you of any sense of esteem, emotional stability, and physical comfort.

A narcissist has the ability to reduce someone who is complex and multifaceted to a simple entity. He can transform his spouse to a nonhuman object. A partner or spouse is diminished not only in the eyes of the narcissist—but also in his or her own eyes. To satisfy the needs of the narcissist, the person providing the supply of admiration and attention will often neglect his or her own existence. They may know that something is sick and wrong with their lives, but they are so entrapped, so much a part of the narcissist's illusion, that they can't cut loose.

Jerry can't ever seem to please Eileen. He can be talking about the weather and Eileen will take exception to something he's said. Her response isn't in the form of irritation, but in seething comments and even rage. During these times, Jerry gets so nervous that he acts and feels like a little boy. He wants to satisfy her, but the more anxious he gets, the more "mistakes" he seems to make.

Eileen is a recovering alcoholic with about five good years of sobriety. Well, maybe not good years, but she hasn't had a drink since 1998. She has narcissistic traits that her treatment counselors attempted to address with her, but to no avail. Although she abused drugs and alcohol for about fifteen years, you'd never know that by looking at her. She's gorgeous, well dressed, and keeps herself very fit. Yet Jerry doesn't worship her the way he used to when they were courting five years ago. Eileen feels she deserves adoration, and if Jerry isn't going to adore her properly, she'll find someone who will. She knows she has treated Jerry cruelly at times, but she's lost respect for him because, as she states, "He's always there and just keeps coming back. What is the matter with him?"

She's just met someone more intriguing at her Twelve Step meeting, and after all, Jerry will be much happier without her.

She remembers when she first met Jerry. He was handsome and in control. She loved his sense of humor and decided that she had to have him. Eileen wooed Jerry and set up an elaborate, seductive web for him. Today she disgustingly recalls how eagerly he took the bait.

SWITCHING OFF

When a narcissist is done with his or her supply, it's over. Just like Eileen, a narcissist is able to delete people and events without the slightest hesitation. This ability to simply switch off is painful and startling to those who have witnessed it. Those on the other side of this phenomenon feel almost as if they had been standing under a shower of incredible love and adoration, then one day the water is turned off without notice—and they are left feeling bare, cold, and bereft. The narcissist moves from expressions of care, love, intense interest, involvement, commitment, protection, and overvaluation to total disregard, disgust, and lack of any interest or emotional involvement.

No one can romance and seduce like a narcissist. If a narcissist sees someone they want, then having "it" becomes a project of massive proportions. This person must be possessed at any cost. Like a spider constructing a web, the narcissist will lure individuals into their trap and eventually become bored, lose respect, or simply destroy them emotionally when they've outlived their usefulness.

Renee had just emerged from a two-year relationship with Yvonne and was ready to get on with her life. Of course, it was Renee's choice to end things; the only thing good in the relationship was sex. There was no more intellectual stimulation because her partner only mimicked what Renee was reading, studying, saying—and it was all too much. Not only that, but Yvonne earned more money and garnered more attention, and it was maddening! Plus. Yvonne didn't deserve it. Day after day, Renee expressed her hurt in raging outbursts and tearful speeches to whoever would listen. She had had quite enough of relationships for quite some time.

Three weeks after her relationship with Yvonne ended, Renee got a glimpse of Sue at a party and was completely smitten by her humor, beauty, and intelligence. Sue was twenty years younger, but this made it even more intriguing for Renee. After her previous relationship, Renee knew that someone younger would look up to her and she intended to foster that dependency.

That night, she couldn't stop thinking about Sue and knew she was in love with her. She'd never felt like this before. Renee knew exactly how to seduce this woman and plotted her moves carefully. She sent cards, gifts, and arranged an elaborate dinner for her at the most expensive restaurant in town. When Sue wasn't "wowed," she flew her to San Francisco and found an exclusive hotel where she spent the weekend showering her with love and affection. Of course, Sue inevitably warmed to this attention and felt as if she'd never been loved like this before. The passion and excitement were so compelling that Sue felt she was living in a dream—and indeed she was.

Three months later, Sue can't understand what

happened to the magic. Now, instead of being showered with love and affection, she can't seem to do anything right. Renee's jealousy has become so out of proportion that Sue has given up spending time with friends or even with family. Consequently, she's isolated herself and made Renee the primary focus of her life. Some evenings, Sue is rewarded for this loyalty and it's as if the old passionate Renee is back. On other days they can be having a cozy dinner, and Sue will be discussing her day at work. Suddenly Renee will take issue with something she's said and become critical and demeaning—and they'll spend the rest of the evening in cold, hostile silence. During these episodes, Renee appears inconsolably hurt and no matter what Sue does, it's not enough. Although Sue hasn't a clue what she has said to alienate Renee, she often winds up apologizing in order to get back in her partner's good graces. The episode often lasts through the next day until Renee decides it's over.

Why would Sue continue to stay in a relationship like this? Part of the reason may be that she had good training in tolerating inappropriate behavior. Sue grew up with a mother who displayed mood fluctuations of mania and depression. Sue never felt comfortable expressing herself at home, and it became clear to her at an early age that neither mom nor dad could tolerate her emotions. As a result, Sue loved the days when mom was funny and manic; they were the happiest of memories. When her mom was depressed, she would mention how useless Sue's dad was, and Sue would relish the fact that she was the only one who could make her mom happy.

How a Narcissist Chooses a Mate

"The brain is a magnificent organ,
it starts from the moment you're born and
doesn't stop until you fall in love."

—PAT LOVE, PSYCHOLOGIST, AUTHOR

Ironically, narcissists tend to choose mates with narcissistic wounds—that is, individuals who themselves received little love and attention as children and don't have the wherewithal to give what they haven't received. These wounded individuals are too often willing to sacrifice themselves in order to get these needs met. In my work with adult children of addicts and alcoholics, it's not unusual to see them in relationships with narcissists or narcissistic addicts. People with borderline personality traits are other potential mates for narcissists. Their fragmented sense of self often propels them into relationships with partners where they can be neither seen nor heard.

Typically, narcissists will choose the following types of mates:

- Another narcissist or someone with narcissistic traits.
- Someone who needs to hide in a relationship.
- A child of a narcissist or a child of an alcoholic/addict.
- Someone who has low self-esteem, feels inadequate, and can be indiscriminately adoring and supportive.
- Someone who is willing to sacrifice his or her personality and endure confinement.

If you're in a relationship with a narcissist, you begin to question your own grip on reality. Indeed, things may have become so bad that you're ashamed to tell friends, family members, or sometimes even a therapist. Since a narcissist denies all negative behavior, it's probable that no one has validated your reality. In short, you may be in a state where you feel confused and doubt your own sanity. The following are questions to ask yourself as you contemplate the possibility that you may be living with a narcissist. As you consider these questions, be aware of your gut reactions and your emotions. The body doesn't lie, and acknowledging these feelings may be the road home to your sanity and your inner wisdom.

- Are you in perpetual doubt as to what is real in your life?
- Have your confidence and self-esteem plummeted since you've been in relationship with this person?
- Do you frequently feel hurt or annoyed that there's no reciprocity, no give and take in your relationship?
- Are you afraid of voicing your opinion or disagreeing for fear of violence or other forms of retaliation?
- Are you reluctant to maintain contact with friends or family because your mate disapproves?
- Have you lost your network of personal or professional friends in order to devote your life to your mate?
- Have you ceased including your partner in your plans because of his or her embarrassing behavior?
- Have you sensed that your partner is devoid of emotion?
- Are you aware that your mate has never made a heartfelt apology or displayed sincere regret for his or her behavior?
- When you are emotionally or physically in pain, does your mate show empathy and warmth?

If the answers to any of these questions resonate with your experience, please be gentle with yourself. Although many mates of narcissists come from families that make them vulnerable to these behaviors, almost anyone can be drawn in by a narcissist's seduction. The most important thing is to save your disappearing self-worth and integrity.

If you care about someone with narcissistic personality

disorder (NPD) or narcissistic traits, you didn't choose that person because you are "sick." Yes, there may be factors in your life that have contributed to your choice of partners. However, there are multifaceted biological and emotional reasons why we choose particular people to love. The bottom line for most of us is that at one point, you cared about this individual and they became important to you.

It's so tragic when I witness men and women blaming themselves for "instigating" narcissistic behavior in their friends, lovers, or business associates. I fully realize that a narcissist has unimaginable persuasive abilities. But just as you wouldn't blame yourself if lightening happened to strike a tree outside, or damaging hail dented your car, it's futile to blame yourself for human behavior that is out of your control. Unfortunately, that's precisely what many people do when faced with the actions of a narcissist. The more you protect the narcissist from facing the consequences of his actions, the less likely it will be that your situation will change. To paraphrase Paul Mason and Randi Kreger in their book *Stop Walking on Eggshells,* the closer you become to a narcissist, the more years you'll spend assuming that you're the source of the lightning, when in fact you're only the lightning rod. (Mason & Kreger, 1998)

THE BONDAGE OF LOVE

A narcissistic bonding pattern is a stranglehold of misery and never ending conflict and occurs when both partners in a relationship have narcissistic wounds. Individuals in this bonding pattern are driven by shame that leads to hypersensitivity and despair. When this occurs, couples find themselves trapped in a stranglehold of misery and intense conflict. For example, it's not uncommon to see an arrogant narcissist in relationship with a shy, closeted narcissist. This symbiotic pairing is a lethal combination and can turn destructive, abusive, and irreparably damaging.

Remember, narcissists are often compelling, and infectiously engaging—that is, as long as you hold them in high regard. If for some reason you're tired, preoccupied, not feeling well, or just plain busy, woe to you! You can become subject to a reign of terror. The narcissist will do what he or she can to get their desires met. They will rage, abuse, become seductive and engaging, and humiliate, and will withhold love from those who don't give them the reflection they need. Sadly, there must be two people to participate in a narcissistic bonding pattern. Both individuals are swept up in a dynamic that feels out of control and destructive. The diagram on page 116 illustrates the bonding pattern in a narcissistic relationship.

The narcissistic bonding pattern begins with *shame*. Both individuals have little, if any, self-esteem and feel defective, deficient, and unworthy. Shame is the underside of narcissism and propels individuals to avoid, attack, or expunge this emotion with devastating results. Both individuals in this relationship have a propensity to react to real or imagined neglect, criticism, or insults. With shame at the core, both the narcissist and his or her mate are reactive and incredibly vulnerable. Despite their grandiosity, narcissists are very thin-skinned, always taking offense and feeling mistreated. This is called *narcissistic vulnerability*.

The next stage of the narcissistic bonding pattern is called *narcissistic expectations*. Both people in this relationship have expectations that come from deficits in early childhood experiences that are painfully transferred to all adult relationships. These expectations fall into two categories: *admiration* and *attention*. Though narcissists crave both, in a relationship there is often one individual who craves one more than the other.

The individual who craves admiration more must have their

The Bonding Pattern in a Narcissistic Relationship

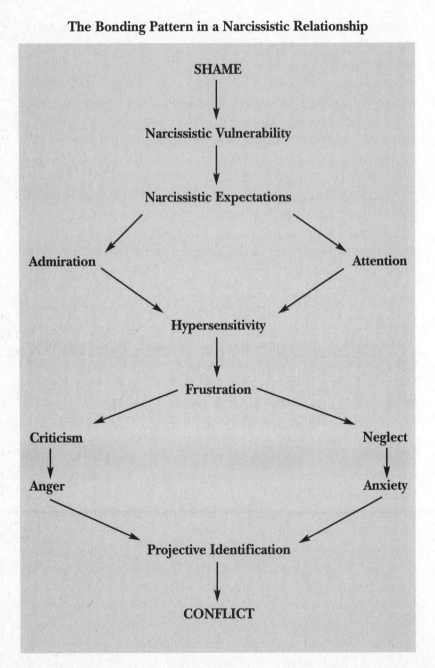

self-esteem inflated and their ego boosted. A constant stream of validation is what they crave. Their lifeblood is gleaning admiration from loved ones, colleagues, and family members. Ironically, this individual will find someone who will put them on a pedestal and make sure that they have a constant flow of adoration. But there are lethal strings attached to this kind of bargain and a covert vow that cannot be broken: If you show adoration and feed my ego, I will give you the kind of attention you've always craved. If I detect the slightest nuance of criticism, I'll ignore you, turn cold, and withhold love and affection.

The adoration that this narcissist requires does not come free. The man or woman who agrees to prop up and inflate their mate's self-esteem demands total and complete attention to their needs, desires, thoughts, and physical appearance. For those who crave attention, the covert agreement with their partner is: You will never be adored the way I can adore you. But if I sense that you're neglecting me, I'll knock you off your pedestal so fast it will make your head spin.

When these individuals get together, what ensues is excruciatingly painful. Both people in this relationship enter the stage of *hypersensitivity*. The partner who demands admiration becomes hypersensitive to any criticism. The mate who demands attention is on mental alert for any hint of inattention or neglect. These two have so many triggers for criticism and neglect that it's as if their relationship is infested with land mines. Simple statements and requests turn into outrageous battles:

- "Your tie is crooked."
- "You made an error when you balanced the checkbook."
- "That woman on TV is so bright, I love listening to her."

Within a short time, their demands become unreasonable.

Each person feels violated, hurt, and perpetually disappointed:

- "You called at 5:10 instead 5:00. You are a cruel and coldhearted person."
- "I want dinner ready when I come in the door, otherwise you're useless. After all, you have nothing better to do with your day."
- "You didn't kiss me like you meant it. I don't care if you're late for work."
- "You obviously enjoyed that movie. I suppose you think Russell Crowe is better looking than I am."

Spending time together becomes a source of hurt, but because narcissistic needs are met intermittently, there is a childlike hope that "perhaps today she'll recognize how special I am." Clearly, no one is going to get their needs met in this relationship, and both partners anticipate *frustration* in their interactions with each other. Time together is spent either processing the pain or avoiding each other to the point of looking elsewhere for another source of supply.

The hurt each experiences turns to revenge as they both endeavor to deprive the other of important needs. How do they do this? The partner who requires admiration treats his mate with *neglect* and disregard. He knows that this has the potential of providing the most severe wounding to his beloved. His mate who craves attention becomes *critical* and condemning. Whether consciously or unconsciously, she fully realizes that criticism is the weapon that will destroy him.

When admiration isn't available, a narcissist often displays *anger* or even *rage*. This rage is raw and frightening and at times, it can turn into physical violence. When this narcissist retaliates by depriving his partner of attention, his mate feels inferior and unlovable, and displays severe *anxiety*. Often, fear of abandonment is at the root of this behavior. The result is a display of childlike behavior that disgusts his or her mate and inevitably provokes more rage. The *conflict* between the two partners becomes so fierce that it makes dinosaur battles look small. What occurs is tragic: this couple can't even discuss the weather without becoming locked in a perpetual pattern of rage and anxiety.

When Max first met Sue, he wasn't particularly impressed with her looks, but her spontaneity and humor were appealing. Max held a prestigious position as vice president of a corporation and Sue's quick wit and lively spirit were refreshing to him. Max grew up with a narcissistic mother and a financially successful father; they were so wrapped up in their lives that neither of them gave Max the validation he deserved. Consequently, Max is insecure about his worth, but you'd never guess this by his demeanor. He seems self-assured and confident, and people depend on him as a leader. He'd been in a couple of relationships before, but so far, every woman had turned out to be a disappointment.

Sue was a successful real estate agent with a history of drug abuse. She grew up in an alcoholic home with five brothers and sisters. As the youngest child, she was the entertainer of the family and everyone doted on her. When she first met Max, she was attracted to his "take charge" manner. She'd never met a man who could walk into a room and garner as much attention and respect. Clearly, he was a man who was in control. With Sue's chaotic childhood and her hectic life, she was drawn to this man who seemed so calm and at ease.

Within a few weeks of dating, they both decided to move in together. This was a huge leap for Max, who loved his own space and resisted sharing it with another person. But Sue seemed to be the exception. She made his life interesting and fun. She adored him and in her eyes he could do no wrong. She listened to his advice, was unconditionally supportive, and deferred to him as the expert in most conversations.

Sue had never experienced the kind of attention she received from Max; he was a real gentleman. Unlike the creeps she'd dated in the past, Max was always complimentary, opened doors, bought her flowers, and would call her every day at work to see how her day was going. He was steady and predictable, and she relished the security she felt in his presence. Two months later, the very qualities that attracted them to each other became the bane of their existence.

One day Max agreed to call Sue at work at a specific time, but because of his hectic day, he decided to put it off. There was much to do to prepare for an important dinner speech he was delivering that evening. After all, because of his important job, Sue needed to understand that she was not always his priority. Besides, he was getting bored with her solicitous manner and missed the excitement he felt when they were first together.

Sue realized that although Max was good at keeping his commitments, lately his attention to her was decreasing. This angered Sue and triggered all the feelings of unpredictability from her past. Forgetting to phone her was the last straw! Instead of telling Max about her disappointment and hurt, she simply canceled the plans for the dinner they were supposed to attend together that evening. She realized that Max was giving an address that night, but he had to pay the consequences of breaking his commitment.

When Max received the phone call from Sue about

the cancellation, he couldn't believe what he was hearing. She gave no explanation and simply said that it was inconvenient for her to attend that evening. When Max hung up the phone, he began to feel the old familiar pain of insecurity and self-doubt. This was an important dinner with business associates and their wives, and he'd been counting on her to be there. If Sue really cared for him, she wouldn't let him down at the last minute like that.

When they met at home that evening, Max went into a rage about how disgusted he was with her behavior, how irresponsible she was, and how he was embarrassed to take her to the dinner anyway because she wasn't that good-looking. Throwing his briefcase across the room, he turned and in an icy voice told her that he was done with her. Sue responded with uncontrollable sobbing and frenetic pacing. Her desperation and anxiety turned into panic. She begged him to give her one more chance and not to end the relationship. Max stormed out of the house yelling that he was tired of her insecurity, and she needed to get some serious help.

The relationship turned from bad to worse when a few days later Max was discussing some article in the newspaper and Sue disagreed with his opinion. Again, Max became angry, then refused to talk to her. Sue became so anxious that she disappeared into the bathroom to take yet another Xanax. The rest of the day Max stayed in a cold silence while Sue tried desperately to apologize for voicing her opinion.

In a short time, the connection they once cherished became one conflict after another. Neither of them could figure out why a relationship that felt so good a few months ago could turn into such a debacle. Their life together was one horrific conflict after the next. Evenings were now spent trying to avoid conflict to the extent that they rarely spoke to each other; when they did, it was about inconsequential details. Max decided they should go to a counselor who could help Sue with her anxiety and insecurity issues. Sue was very agreeable and saw it as a chance to help Max with his control and anger problems.

HOLD THAT FEELING AND I'LL EXPRESS IT FOR YOU: PROJECTIONS AND DISTORTIONS

Max and Sue are locked in a bonding pattern of anxiety and anger. They are unable to move out of the gridlock that has made their life together constraining and miserable. Perhaps you noticed that when Sue first changed plans for the date she was feeling angry. When Max first heard of the change in plans he felt insecure and demeaned. However, when they're together, it's Sue who expresses the insecurity and Max who expresses the anger. In other words, they blame each other for the emotions they each initially held. This dynamic is called *projective identification* (Ogden, 1993): what is emotionally unacceptable is unconsciously discarded and projected to another. In a narcissistic bonding pattern, each person will blame the partner for the very emotions or behaviors they themselves possess. Projective identification is a script that is played by two. The process is insidious and involves psychologically transferring a piece of oneself onto another and then inducing the other to behave in accordance with the projection. It is not unusual in these situations to see couples that cannot tolerate each other because they carry each other's most unacceptable and intolerable qualities.

In the example of Sue and Max, Sue cannot bear her feelings of anger and unconsciously provokes Max to be angry with her. In fact, Sue declares that Max really needs help with his anger, when, ironically, anger is Sue's first response to lack of attention. Max complains that Sue's insecurity is driving him mad, when it's Max who has the initial response of insecurity and self-doubt that he cannot tolerate. He proceeds to behave in ways that trigger Sue's deepest fears and anxieties, and then blames her for this response. Max then resorts to name-calling and abusive behavior, true to form for an individual with a narcissistic injury.

In desperation, Sue has purchased hundreds of dollars of books trying to figure out what's wrong with their relationship and what she can do to be a better partner to Max. Sadly, relationship books aren't going to resolve this painful dynamic. They may provide Sue with some insight, teach her how men and women communicate differently, or explain what a woman must do to win a man's heart. Unfortunately, however, people don't change by learning more information.

The only way to break a bonding pattern is through honest vulnerability. If Sue could have communicated to Max about her disappointment and hurt when he didn't call her, or if Max could have told Sue how insecure he felt when she canceled plans with no explanation, their evening may not have been a catastrophe. However, honesty and vulnerability are not within the realm of possibility for narcissists who are driven by shame. For both Sue and Max, it will take self-reflection, awareness, and the painstaking work of building a non-defensive sense of self in the context of an empathic, caring, therapeutic relationship.

DEALING WITH DIFFERENT
NARCISSISTIC BEHAVIOR TYPES

Although there are many types of narcissistic behaviors, the spouses and partners with whom I've worked through the years are particularly perplexed about how to handle the exaggerated jealousy and the fearsome bullying. The following are suggestions that can be used when you encounter these behaviors in your relationship:

The Jealous Narcissist

Your only protection is the plain truth. Tell it once and never submit to cross-examination. This is easy to say, but hard to do. It's important to state your boundaries ahead of time so there are no surprises. "I'm completely loyal to you and have nothing to hide. When you ask me where I was and what I was doing, I will tell you once. If you keep questioning me, I will excuse myself and leave the room."

Since jealousy is a quality that's inherent to pathological narcissism, it's likely that this behavior will continue. With this in mind, it's crucial that you take care of yourself by developing the skills to firmly and respectfully end the conversation and leave the room.

Jealousy can trigger narcissistic rage and violence, and when partners hang around for a jealous outburst, it can be dangerous. Threatening to call the police is of no help if you're not willing to follow through. In fact, it makes you look foolish in the eyes of a narcissist. If you're being threatened with physical violence or touched in anger, it's time to call the authorities. If you have children, then this is an absolute necessity.

The Bullying Narcissist

Don't undermine yourself by thinking you're going to get a bullying narcissist to realize how badly they've made you feel. It's not going to happen. Resist at all costs the temptation to engage in an angry tirade or participate in revenge. This is your emotional/limbic brain working overtime (see pages 194–195). Instead you can learn to deflect the rage or bullying. Bullies get a lot of mileage out of threats. For example, in the workplace it's more likely that this narcissist will drive you to leave rather than fire you. To cope with bullies, you have to do what they cannot do: stay cool and keep your wits about you.

Ask for time to think about what they are saying. This communicates that you're taking the comments seriously. No matter what, take the time to think before you respond.

Think about what you want to happen. While you're taking a minute to think, go over the possible outcomes. Immediately discard any strategy that will force this person to admit you're right and back down.

Ask the bully to slow down because you want to understand him—reducing the speed of his words will also reduce the volume. It will also communicate that you really want to know what he is saying.

These same narcissistic behaviors occur in women as well as men. Bullying, jealousy, and emotional violence are not exclusive to males. To underestimate a female narcissist in her ability to inflict pain in her personal and professional relationships is a mistake. The following chapter illumines the pattern of female narcissists and will hopefully broaden the perspective of those trying to understand how this disorder manifests in women.

The Narcissist Woman

*"Mirror, mirror on the wall, who's the
fairest of them all?"*

*I*n our society, we can more easily spot a narcissistic
man—those intelligent, self-confident, and ultimately
uncaring and unfaithful men who seem at first to be so
exciting. (Campbell, 2005) Even though men are diagnosed
more often than women (75 percent) with narcissism or narcissistic tendencies, women are by no means exempt from this
phenomenon. Clinicians are biased. Studies show, for
example, that mental health professionals tend to diagnose
borderline personality disorder in women more often than
men, even when patient profiles are identical except for the
gender of the patient. Most surveys find that narcissism is just
as common in women. The characteristics may show up differently in women and may be more challenging to spot, but
females have narcissistic wounds just as males do. Even though

psychiatrists are more likely to diagnose a woman with histrionic or borderline personality disorder than with narcissism, it would be a mistake not to recognize the female narcissist and the chaos she causes to the partners, children, friends, and others in her life.

A female narcissist can be a wife, mother, sister, or daughter. And if the world revolves around her, she is happy. Seemingly significant people in her life are really no more than objects who give her what she wants and needs: love, admiration, money, encouragement, support, accolades, and anything in between. (Matiatos, 2002) She can be young or old, pretty or not, and like her male counterpart her voice takes on exactly the right tone that's needed to seduce her prey: demanding; filled with a sense of unearned entitlement; soft and seductive; coolly intellectual; full of disdain; or extremely calculating.

The narcissistic female will use a partner in shrewd and cold ways. She can't or won't show remorse and will not apologize for even the most egregious behavior. If a relationship turns out to be a shipwreck of conflict, she'll walk away from it with barely a bruise. If she loses a partner, she may seem authentically upset, angry, or anxious, but she will then proceed almost immediately into the next relationship. These women can be ruthless and use whatever means they have in order to get their needs met, including helplessness, calculated vulnerability, seduction, affected warmth, abuse, brainwashing, and physical abuse. Female narcissists turn the art of seduction into a frightening art form. Whether her audience is gay or straight, this woman has no shame when it comes to using her charms.

The victims of narcissistic women are frequently the ones over which she has the most power—her family. Criticizing, verbally abusing, and sometimes physically assaulting, she can't allow them to be too successful or too happy. Ironically, the more she loves them, the more she reduces them to nothing. (Potter-Efron, 2002) The narcissistic mother requires a perfect child to mirror her perfection. If her children disappoint her in some way by their appearance, gender, or some other flaw, the mother will feel defective, which in turn triggers shame and rage.

A narcissistic mother will likely view her daughter both as an extension of herself and as a competitive adversary. She will project the good/bad mother onto her child and enter into abusive conflict with her. When her child is useful to her or when she's in public with her child, the narcissistic woman becomes the "good" mother and exhibits warmth and caring. The "bad" mother surfaces when the child doesn't meet her needs. This occurs most often in the privacy of the home where she becomes caustic, angry, and demeaning. A child will experience confusion and dissonance when the same behavior that elicited praise in public becomes a source of ridicule at home. This behavior can take place between mothers and sons as well, but daughters seem to be the primary targets for this behavior.

In fact, many fairy tales are shot through with strands of narcissistic women who must destroy their female daughters or stepdaughters. From the stories of Snow White to Cinderella, these tales are replete with young women who must flee their narcissistic guardians only to enter into questionable relationships with flawed dwarves (Sleepy, Bashful, Dopey, and so forth) or supposed princes as a means of escape. (Joslin, 2008)

It's easier for a woman to think of her children as her extensions because her ongoing interaction with them is both more intensive and more extensive. (This means that the male narcissist is more likely to regard his children as a nuisance than as a source of rewarding narcissist supply—especially as they grow and become autonomous). Through insidious indoctrination, guilt, emotional sanctions, deprivation, and other psychological mechanisms, the narcissistic mother fosters in her children a dependency that cannot be easily unraveled. (Matiatos, 2002)

DIFFERENCES IN
FEMALE NARCISSIST STYLES

If a woman is a somatic narcissist, she will be preoccupied with her appearance and feel entitled to drive herself and her family into debt in order to adorn herself properly. This type of narcissistic woman shows no regret about spending beyond her means, or beyond anyone else's either. She feels as if it's her spouse's obligation to support her in a luxurious manner.

Incidentally, the difference between compulsive shopping and narcissistic buying is a matter of shame versus shameless-ness. Most compulsive shoppers feel a sense of deep shame after they return home with their purchases or receive the bill. They realize they have a problem but are unable to stop. Narcissistic women don't think they have a problem, haven't the slightest inclination to stop, and will shrewdly undermine anyone who gets in their way.

The somatic female narcissist may react in an out-of-control manner to slight weight gains, scrapes, bruises, or an uneven sun tan. She'll parade her body unabashedly at the gym, at the office, and at home. If her partner, children, or friends don't feed her exactly the right compliments, she will obsess about it and repay them by withholding love, spewing vitriol, or col-lapsing in a flood of tears and self-pity.

If a female is a cerebral narcissist, she might exploit her gen-der and her intellet to increase her professional status. For ex-ample, although she might care little about women's rights, she'll use this issue to achieve notoriety and fame. She'll de-fend the underdog and feel herself to be part of this "victim-ized" group while treating the women in her life with disrespect or neglect.

In a relationship, she will choose someone who meets her intellectual standards, then proceed to devalue this person.

This woman will talk circles around anyone and make sure others are constantly aware of her degrees, her acumen, and her superiority. She will idealize a heterosexual partner then emasculate him. She will seduce a female partner, display her like a prize, and then hide her away until it's convenient to let her out of the closet. If her partner isn't as "out" as she would like, the cerebral narcissist will lecture, present the latest research, threaten, and argue until her partner finally relents. Then one day, the narcissistic female will suddenly want to hide this woman, persuading her not to participate in social functions or making sure she stays invisible in other ways.

Does society encourage narcissistic behavior in women? Most young women learn as early as age eleven or twelve that if they wear a short skirt, men will hover around them offering attention, gifts, and compliments. In our culture beauty is power. Ask any schoolteacher who has witnessed an attractive, otherwise normal, twelve-year-old young woman become self-centered by age fourteen, while a less attractive teenager who dresses in ordinary clothing, or has minor flaws to her complexion or body becomes quickly ostracized as a pariah.

Many women raised in this culture also have to grapple with the phenomenon of "superwoman," the female who has a successful career and also comes home at night to be a superb wife, lover, mother, and homemaker. Here the therapeutic maneuver must be toward the acceptance of being merely human. Someplace between "'superwoman'" and the narcissistic abandonment of the nurturing role (that is, "doing our own thing") there is a middle ground: doing the best one can, accepting one's own limits, doing for others without paying too heavy a price, and doing for oneself without abandoning the needs of others. (Potter-Efron, 1989)

Linda Marks, M.S.M., says that each gender has a different and corresponding response to a narcissistic wound. The stereotypic male response is, "These people can't take care of me, so I will become big and strong and take care of myself. I don't need anyone." The stereotypic female response is, "I can't make it on my own. I'll find someone who can protect me, because I don't have the power to do it by myself." (Marks, 2007)

The real insidiousness of female narcissism may be that it can be disguised in many ways that don't fit the stereotypic models we've been discussing here. This is most evident with women in the business world, but the female narcissist also can be a Brownie Scout troop leader, a member of the Junior League, or the mother down the block.

How Do You Spot a Narcissistic Woman?

"She was the only woman I ever knew that could strut while sitting down."

—Bob Brissette, addiction counselor,
and renowned AA speaker

You can tell a woman has narcissistic traits when she feels good about herself only if she feels she is better than you. She must be prettier, smarter, a greater cook, or a better mother than any other woman in her life. If there's a hint that you may exceed her in any area, her charm turns to a cold shoulder or irritation bordering on contempt. Jealousy is a huge issue. She is unaware of her own bitter envy, even as it raises its ugly head to plot your demise. This can involve slipping a well-placed bad word or two about you to the boss, or viciously gossiping about you to the neighbors. If she is an employer, she can be ruthless in removing anyone she feels is a threat to her superiority or beauty. Whatever you do for her, it is never enough. If you're a friend, partner, or business colleague, you'll find yourself obsessing and anxious about what she will require of you today.

When caught with her vigilant guard down, she is not nice. She is often impatient, short, arrogant, and condescending and in a near chronic bad mood. Like the male narcissist, her moods are unpredictable. The energy demands of being "on" are too great, especially when she is frustrated. And when her frustration slips away from her, it spills onto anybody unfortunate enough to be in the way.

The Diva

At one time, divas were celebrated as larger than life. They strode the world's opera stages, beguiling their adoring audiences with magnificent voices and onstage and offstage melodrama. We forgave their sense of entitlement because it seemed earned due to their extraordinary talent. Today, we have divas that are filled with "attitude" that is rarely backed up by anything *other* than a sense of entitlement.

Divas are drama queens. Starting every sentence with "Oh my God, you'll never guess what happened," the diva's life is one of extremes, good or bad. She goes from crisis to crisis, feeding off chaos. Whether she's breaking up with her boyfriend for the third time this week, or fretting that the newly found wrinkle on her face is a sign of premature aging, nothing just happens to this person—it's always a *catastrophe!* She simply wears us out.

Stores and restaurants are a diva's prime stomping grounds. That's where you hear: "What about that table?" "I want to sit there!" "Take that away immediately. I don't want it!" There is no grace and no sense of embarrassment. These are women who can turn on disingenuous sweetness at a moment's notice, depending on what they need or who they're trying to impress. (I once did some couples therapy with a high-powered woman and her husband. I noticed that during our sessions she was outrageously rude and demeaning to her husband while at the same time being honey-voiced and seductive with me.)

Of course everyone has bad days, when a demeaning waiter or waitress dismisses us, or we encounter a salesperson with the personality of Attila the Hun. A bad encounter coupled with a miserable day at work or home makes containing our reactions beyond challenging. During those experiences, many of us want to throw a fit and put these people in their place. There are those of us who can pull ourselves together and either walk away or maintain our dignity in some way. However, for women with narcissistic wounds, there is no containment or respect for the boundaries of others.

Anne Taylor Fleming, a nationally recognized journalist and essayist, has created a list entitled "You Know You're a Diva When . . .":

- You raise your voice at a waitress or waiter and set off a collective cringe among diners at your table.
- You persist in screeching into your cell phone in a public place despite the reactions from people around you.
- You interrupt a salesclerk who is helping someone else and demand instant attention.
- You leave the house with a teacup-sized dog under your arm and allow it to yap at everyone while you coo at it.
- You have a fender bender and flee the scene of the crime with a shrug of your shoulders.
- You stamp your stilettos and get huffy when you don't get seated at the table of your choice.
- You cut in front of people in a line at the bank or at the movies while assuming a holier-than-thou posture. (Fleming, 2006)

PART 3

THE NARCISSISTIC CLIENT

Narcissus in Wonderland: The Narcissistic Addict

*L*ewis Carroll's fable for children, *Alice's Adventures in Wonderland,* tells about a young woman who swallows a magic pill and drops down a rabbit hole into a strange and wondrous land. If we link that tale to the myth of Narcissus, who is captivated by his own self-image, we have a description of the narcissistic addict: a man or woman who is both narcissistically disordered and lost in a version of wonderland. For some men and women, addiction is characterized by an insatiable desire to recover an infantile state of gratification, which certainly can't be filled in reality—only in "wonderland." (Ulman & Paul, 2006; Joslin, 2008)

No one knows exactly how addiction occurs. But narcissists are set up for addictive behavior as their true self goes into hiding at an early age in order to please a parent figure and to survive. Emerging in its place is a false self that writes checks of bravado and grandiosity from an empty bank account.

Narcissists come to believe that they *are* their false self, but nothing can stop their pernicious sense of shame from bleeding into their reality. With the discovery of mind-altering substances and compulsive behaviors, the painful cracks between the shame and the false self are filled perfectly—if only momentarily—to create a smooth shiny surface: a mirror! And just like Narcissus, as addicts become transfixed on that silvery mirror, they are transported to a warm, safe, and nurturing place where no one can cause them pain. As Phil Joslin, an addiction counselor in London writes, "So powerful is the draw to the silvery pool of the drug that I no longer need food, shelter, or warmth . . . And slowly, day by day I pine and wither away and die." (Joslin, 2008)

Eventually the tables are turned, however, and the drug that once provided the narcissist with control over unwanted emotions now begins to control the narcissist. In order for sobriety and recovery to occur, the treatment counselor must develop a relationship with the shameful true self, much to the chagrin of the narcissistic patient. The addiction counselor is unconsciously threatened to avoid making waves in the "pool." Any ripples will fracture the reflection and the narcissistic addict's sense of self. Any interventions will be attacked, or ignored. Yet this is precisely the type of therapeutic relationship that is required to begin the path of healing.

It makes perfect sense why a narcissist would turn to alcohol, drugs, or compulsive behavior for comfort. Shame and addiction are natural partners and shame is at the root of compulsive behavior. (Kaufman, 1992) The more internal shame a person feels, the more likely he will be attracted to anything that promises relief from pain and emptiness. Since the core emotion of a narcissist is shame, they are at high risk for addiction to substances ranging from sex to drugs to alcohol.

Narcissistic personality disorder (NPD) often leads to use of drugs, particularly stimulants. A shy person with NPD may depend on drugs or alcohol to relieve her social anxiety, while others use steroids to boost their confidence in physical perfection. Without alcohol and drugs, a person with NPD may believe that others are overly critical or do not adequately appreciate his or her good qualities.

A majority of individuals with NPD, perhaps up to 50 percent, are substance abusers. (Wallach & Wallach 1983) And many addicts are themselves raised by addicts. Research shows that consistency, boundaries, safety, and respect are often missing in these families. According to Dr. Gary Forrest, executive director of the International Academy of Behavioral Medicine, alcoholics have a history of experiencing profound narcissistic need and deprivation in their families. Suffice it to say that many alcoholics and addicts have narcissistic traits that manifest in several ways and make recovery challenging. (Forrest, 1994)

In families where alcoholism exists, the entire family adjusts to the behavior of the addict/alcoholic. Indeed, the family system is not a child-centered home, but an alcoholic-centered home. Everyone surrounding the addict props up his ego, hides his behavior from the world, and is consumed with not upsetting him lest he start using again. His disappointment brings wrath, he makes plans with children and doesn't keep them, and his need for the drug or alcohol becomes his primary relationship. You can see by this short description that the center of family attention is the alcoholic. And this family dynamic can go on for years! How does one step away from the spotlight and become one of the many addicts trying to get sober in treatment or in a Twelve Step program? Recovery is a humbling experience and the notion of powerlessness over one's addiction certainly does not come easy to those with narcissistic traits.

Many addicts believe that they deserve special treatment simply because they exist. If they go to treatment, they expect to be placed on a pedestal where they can be worshipped and adored. They think it's obvious that they're better than anyone else. When others don't seem to have that reaction to them, some addicts become incensed; others ignore criticism rather than get angry because they do not respect those who can't appreciate them. These are the types of patients who are egotistical to the point that counselors feel as if they're making no headway with them. Unfortunately, these characteristics aren't uncommon; they are part of the experience in treating and living with addicts/alcoholics. And these characteristics don't disappear in sobriety or recovery. In fact, they are exacerbated and cause endless misery to those around them. Confronting the behaviors of false pride, conceit, haughtiness, and entitlement must be part of a treatment program if there is to be sobriety, let alone recovery.

KING AND QUEEN BABIES

"Before you begin treatment,
may I adjust your crown?"

Having consulted with treatment centers for many years, I'm profoundly aware of the term "King Baby." Although the image conjured up by this phrase is someone who's arrogant, snobbish, demanding, and aloof, the truth is that these are the very men who feel painfully inferior inside. In fact, the more a person displays this "kingly" behavior, the more second-rate he feels. These addicts/alcoholics are hiding tremendous shame with their pride. (Potter-Efron & Potter-Efron, 1989]

Feelings of entitlement, grandiosity, and contempt are such a part of the disease of addiction that a diagnosis of NPD is difficult to make. For someone living with a narcissistic addict or alcoholic, the devastation caused by addiction coupled with narcissistic traits feels insurmountable.

Bob Brissette, a Hazelden treatment counselor and celebrated speaker on alcoholism, gave the following description of "King Baby" (Brissette, 1971):

> Like babies, alcoholics assume that the world is our little private oyster. We tyrannize our homes, our wives, and our children: we demand meals to be served before there has been an opportunity to prepare them. Then we throw tantrums if everything isn't done thoroughly. We demand that food be of our choice, not the family's choice. We demand that our TV program be tuned in, not the family's program. And we deserve this, we tell ourselves—didn't we work hard all day down at the office? What if we did have five coffee breaks, a three-martini lunch that lasted 'til 2:45, and a couple of long, warm counseling sessions with that pretty girl employee who told us how kind and understanding we were. . . . We're adept at twisting knives, cutting people up and humiliating them and making them frightened, insecure about our jobs. And we do this because it makes us feel better: it makes us feel more powerful.

An addict has difficulty coping with the normal frustrations of life. The "king," however, because of his feeling of omnipotence and impatience, is constantly creating unnecessary roadblocks by storming ahead despite the cost. (Tiebout, 1953) The narcissistic alcoholic shouldn't have to be bothered with recovery and may see the fellowship as trivial and boring; that is, unless he's in charge. He has little staying power for sobriety and expects quick results. Since recovery is one day at a time, and the surrender to the notion of powerlessness is tantamount to recovery, the prognosis is poor.

The king baby has a female counterpart called the "queen." She's easy to recognize. She might sweep into the room a halfhour late and everyone must drop what they're doing and notice her. Her great need is to be the constant center of attention wherever she is. Frequently, she speaks and laughs in a loud and what she thinks is an arresting, interesting way—but it isn't. If the queen feels like granting you a sexual favor, you are expected to be grateful to her to your death for having had the privilege of bedding her. She demands absolute respect from her family and children. She whines and whimpers when all of her demands are not met promptly. She feels entitled to proper gratitude for your having the privilege of serving her.

The queen is in deadly competition with her daughters. When they get to be teenagers and she's starting to sag a little, an ugly, hateful battle develops between her and her children. Like the king, she sees other people as things, not as human beings or equals. To her, people are objects to be terrorized, bullied, and manipulated into loving, serving, and being loyal to her.

BARRIERS TO RECOVERY

A barrier to recovery for women, one that is discussed all too infrequently, is anger or rage, which simmers beneath the surface of many narcissistic female alcoholics. (Rolls, 1995) Defense against strong feelings of shame include perfectionism, entitlement, and feelings of rage. But expression of overt anger and resentment is not acceptable and might be difficult for the narcissistic woman in treatment. (Potter-Efron, 2002) Research shows that compared to men, women entering treatment carry more shame and enter treatment at later stages of the disease. Suffice it to say that there are a number of highly distressed alcohol women who haven't been able to bring themselves to treatment. Add this to the grandiosity and pride of the narcissistic female and you have a shameful alcoholic/addict who will likely defend against getting any help until her disease becomes acute.

Female addicts/alcoholics with narcissistic partners present a different set of issues that might make sobriety and recovery unattainable. Women living with narcissistic partners often have a high tolerance for abuse and may medicate with alcohol to tolerate their relationships. For these women, admitting a drinking problem would only incur ridicule and shame. If they do enter treatment, their primary focus will likely be on getting sober so that their narcissistic partner will remain with them. After treatment, these women will likely turn their attention back to their partners and allow him or her to dictate whether she'll remain sober or not. Alcoholics don't recover in isolation. It's likely that a narcissistic partner will humiliate her if she attends Alcoholics Anonymous. If her narcissistic partner doesn't support her sobriety and insists that she drink or use drugs with him or her, then her abstinence will be short-lived.

In treatment, a narcissistic addict/alcoholic will consider himself above the rules and proceed to break them without remorse. Group members and even counselors may resign themselves to this behavior in order to avoid his wrath. The narcissistic addict will be intolerant and abusive to those who disagree with him or point out his "character defects." Yet this same individual can be affable, cooperative, and completely disarming in order to win you over and get narcissistic supply. Masters of manipulation, they will steer any group process in their direction and leave even the most competent clinician baffled as to what occurred.

Sadly, a narcissist may complete the treatment process and not have absorbed anything. Part of the reason is that the qualities of both addiction and narcissism make it possible for him or her to turn in a convincing, magnificent performance. In other words, these individuals can use the appropriate recovery vernacular, lie about their progress, and generally manipulate counselors into believing that they're sincerely interested in what's being said. In addition, interrupting the denial dynamic of a narcissistic addict is like breaking into Fort Knox. When confronted with his behavior, a narcissistic addict will twist and manipulate his explanation like an artist. He may, for example, claim to be using drugs in order to conduct firsthand research for the benefit of humanity. Or he will give you explicit data that explains how his substance abuse isn't hurting anyone and provides him with enhanced creativity and productivity.

Addiction professionals know that relapse is very often a part of recovery. However, should the narcissist relapse—an almost certain occurrence—she will feel ashamed about admitting her fallibility, need for emotional sustenance, and impotence. Subsequently, she is likely to avoid treatment altogether and will convince herself that now, having succeeded once in getting rid of her addiction, she is self-sufficient and omniscient.

A caution to treatment counselors: Researchers in the field of addiction, Drs. Lisa Najavitz and Roger Weiss (Najavitz & Weiss, 2002) report that negative counter transference is more common in alcoholism than in any other mental illness. Counter transference refers to unresolved and/or unconscious conflicts within the therapist, which are triggered by the patient. Particularly with a narcissistic addict/alcoholic, the tendency to project blame, cast dispersions, belittle, and humiliate are not uncommon. The reason we need to do our own work and avail ourselves of supervision is so we become more aware of those lost areas of ourselves and allow them to become available to our consciousness in order to better help our clients.

Finally, at heart, all addicts are self-destructive, self-defeating, and self-loathing. In other words: addicts are predominantly masochists while narcissists, in contrast, are sadists. Consequently, the prognosis for narcissistic addicts is poor, but *not* hopeless.

Narcissists and AA

*"The only thing you need to know about God
is that you're not him."*

—Twelve Step Aphorism

According to the Center for Substance Abuse Treatment, Twelve Step programs are often helpful for patients with addiction and narcissistic personality disorder. (CSAT, 1994) In fact, contrary to common belief, it's altogether possible for narcissistic addicts to actively engage in Twelve Step programs. With time, participating in the fellowship can bring about clear, empathic mirroring in which the true self can emerge from hiding and slowly feel accepted as he or she comes into the world. After all, practicing the twelve steps can transform shame into guilt through the admission of powerlessness rather than defectiveness. This has the possibility through time of altering the vicious cycle of defensiveness and allowing the narcissist to become more aware of his or her limits.

There are narcissists, however, who skew the program to meet their need for narcissistic supply. They are the people who make all the meetings and seem to know all the answers (even though they've only participated for a couple of weeks). Everyone tells them how great they are, and how many people they've helped. They speak up at meetings and are always ready to give advice. You see, this venue can be the perfect hunting ground for narcissistic supply—an unending source of admiration and attention. Why is this source unending? Because if one group becomes "stale," a man or woman can simply go to another group, soaking up more praise and even preying on new, vulnerable members. Sadly, this obviously defeats the purpose and healing intent of these meetings. What is even more paradoxical is that despite their endless stream of advice, these are men and women who often can't manage to stay sober.

No matter what propels a narcissist to continue participating in the fellowship of AA, as long they attend meetings there's always the slight chance they will get some empathic healing and continued sobriety. This is particularly true if they are fortunate enough to find sponsorship with someone who has some good years of recovery from addiction and narcissistic wounds.

Narcissism:
A Difficult Diagnosis

*M*ental disorders are organized in the *Diagnostic and Statistical Manual of Mental Disorders* (DSM) into categories. Axis II is the grouping for underlying pervasive or personality conditions like narcissism. The American Psychiatric Association estimates that only one in one hundred meet the criteria for the severe form of narcissism—narcissistic personality disorder (NPD). Many of these men and women never come to the attention of professionals because they don't believe they have a problem and have become adept at blaming others for their behavior.

Considerable overlap between the characteristics of different personality disorders makes diagnosis of NPD a challenge. In fact, NPD is considered to have one of the highest rates of diagnostic overlap among the Axis II disorders. (Gunderson, Ronningstam, & Smith, 1991) For example, if you listen to spouses of narcissists or spouses with partners who have borderline personality disorder (BPD) or antisocial personality disorder (ASPD), the way in which they describe their partners can sound disturbingly alike. In fact, the presenting symptoms are so comparable that it can be difficult to make an accurate diagnosis.

Personality disorders such as BPD and NPD are organized in cluster groups according to the degree of their similarity. Personality disorders such as narcissism are included in Cluster B—the category of dramatic, emotional, or erratic disorders that includes:

- Antisocial Personality
- Borderline Personality
- Histrionic Personality
- Narcissistic Personality

The need for constant attention typifies individuals with a histrionic personality disorder. However, narcissists can behave in very similar ways, particularly a somatic narcissist who can become hysterical and dramatic when it comes to insults or the slightest cut or bruise to the body. One significant difference between these two disorders is that the histrionic individual is capable of warmth, dependency, genuine concern, and commitment, while the narcissist is more controlled, calculating, cold, and aggressive. (Kernberg, 2000; Millon et al, 2004)

Antisocial personality disorder is differentiated from NPD by the ASPD's willingness to use physical violence (psychopaths fall under this category). Narcissists are less likely to commit violent crimes (Kernberg, 2000; Vaknin, 2007).

Narcissists, for example, react to criticism emotionally, while those with antisocial disorders are much more likely to act out physically. A narcissist's primary style is using more subtle, manipulative, emotional torture. (Ronningstam, 2005) Also, there is a distinction between psychopaths who have no conscience and therefore no need for self-deception, and cruel narcissists who use self-deception to keep the emotional consequences out of their awareness.

Grandiosity, lack of empathy, and exploitative interpersonal relations are not exclusive to NPDs, nor is the need to be seen as special or unique. You will find narcissists, as well as those with ASPD, manipulating, lying, and displaying a complete lack of concern for anyone but themselves. And the effects they have on others close to them are strikingly similar. Thus, a person with NPD can possess traits of each of the Cluster B disorders; in psychiatric lingo this is referred to as *comorbidity*. For example, when you look at some of the behaviors of BPD, they can appear very similar to those of a narcissist:

Traits of Borderline Personality Disorder (BPD)

- Difficulty controlling emotions or impulses.
- Frequent, dramatic changes in mood, opinions, and plans.
- Stormy relationships involving frequent, intense anger (including the possibility of physical violence).
- Fear of being alone despite a tendency to push people away.
- Feeling of emptiness inside.
- Suicide attempts or self-mutilation.

SHAME: THE UNDERSIDE OF NARCISSISM

Despite the similarities between NPD and BPD, they have distinctly different characteristics as well. The diagnosis of NPD is typically made based on the absence of certain behaviors. For instance, NPDs have a more solid, organized sense of self, with fewer tendencies to regressive fragmentation. Fragmentation means the dread of the loss of sense of self or the breakdown of stability. BPD patients have a more poorly integrated self and a risk for the occurrence of psychotic-like states. When fears of fragmentation exist, people do not have the "luxury" of registering shame; A degree of self-cohesion or internal structure are necessary to even recognize "shame." For narcissists, however, shame is their central affective experience. (Morrison, 1997) Due to a higher level of cohesiveness, NPDs are associated with greater tolerance for aloneness and with better employment records, impulse control, and anxiety tolerance. People with BPD, due to their lower level of cohesiveness, are associated more with self-mutilation and persistent rage. (Akhtar, 2008)

The primary distinction between NPD and BPD lies in the narcissist's core of shame. Dr. Andrew Morrison, in his book entitled *Shame, the Underside of Narcissism* (Morrison, 1997) points out that shame is the base emotion for narcissists; in fact, rage, contempt, and blame are only vehicles used to expunge this shame because it's so intolerable. This is hard to comprehend if you've lived with a narcissist. How can one with such bravado, grandiosity, and arrogance feel worthless and despicable?

People who have true self-esteem and personal integrity don't behave in arrogant ways. These positive qualities show up in a quiet confidence that needs no explanation or boasting about. Contrast that with a narcissist who, with all his bluster, feels deficient and inadequate, worthless and inferior. A narcissist knows that at his core he is a liar and an imposter. At some level, he feels his life has been a hoax, a waste. These beliefs bring up shame—the most painful emotion of them all. (Almaas, 2004)

While narcissists suffer from shame, their reactions are most often shameless. Shameless people stand aloof from others and appear to be indifferent to anything but praise. The truth is that narcissists are hiding tremendous shame with their pride. (Potter-Efron & Potter-Efron, 1989) Narcissists develop defensive strategies to sidestep shame: rage, perfectionism, arrogance, and even exhibitionism. When these defenses work, narcissists can convince themselves that they have nothing to feel ashamed of. The price they pay, however, is to be cut off both from reality and from human intimacy. You see, while shame involves the feeling of internal defectiveness, it also signals a powerful longing for connection.

When issues of internal shame are present, typically individuals will act in one of four ways: withdraw, compulsively avoid, attack self, or attack others, as shown in the diagram below.

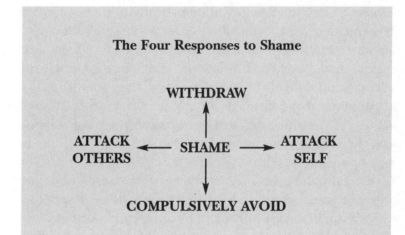

WITHDRAWAL. The narcissist isolates from others and goes into emotional hiding. For narcissists, this can take the form of withholding love or attention. For those on the receiving end, it feels as if you've been abruptly locked out of the house on a brutally cold day with no possibility of getting in. It's a cruel withholding that's extraordinarily wounding.

COMPULSIVELY AVOID. The narcissist turns to alcohol, drugs, or other compulsive behaviors like gambling, sexual acting out, or even shopping. The link between narcissism and addiction has been well documented. For narcissists, using drugs or alcohol to self-medicate is a remedy for alleviating shame.

ATTACK SELF. The narcissist engages in self-mutilation by vicious internal dialogues.

ATTACK OTHERS. The narcissist typically attacks other in a variety of ways in order to obliterate his own shame.

A narcissist must control people and his surroundings in order to keep from feeling the shame of being an imposter. His fervent goal is to manage the impressions that others have of him. Thus, to avoid feeling the shame of his inadequacy, a narcissist is compelled to influence others' perceptions by manipulating and controlling information, dominating a situation, and being the center of attention. He will do whatever it takes to avoid feeling shame. And if, despite his efforts, a narcissist does feel this excruciating shame, he will attempt to purge the shame through attacks on objects, living or inanimate. It's not uncommon to see a narcissist throw objects, kick the wall, or slam doors when they are in the middle of a rage episode.

Generally, the relational dynamic of a narcissist is also quite different when compared to those with BPD. A narcissist expects you to revolve around her universe and worship her as a goddess. In contrast, the individual with a borderline personality wraps her universe *around you,* as if to *fuse* with her very existence—*you* are her universe.

Another symptom of BPD is self-mutilation. A person with this disorder feels such intense angst, coupled with emptiness, that cutting or otherwise harming her body provides relief from the internal pain. In contrast, narcissists don't typically mutilate their bodies: somatic narcissists would find this unfathomable and cerebral narcissists would think it ludicrous. Besides, the narcissist's defense usually is to "mutilate" others emotionally.

In addition, narcissists, unlike those with BPD, rarely commit suicide. Narcissists may have suicidal ideation and even brag about an ingenious suicidal plan, but they rarely commit a suicidal act. Narcissists may react to extreme stress by becoming temporarily suicidal but committing suicide truly runs against their grain.

Research shows that narcissists also are developmentally a bit better off than someone with BPD (Schore, 1994) A person with BPD has an arrested emotional development that mental health professionals set below the age of twelve months; those with NPD have an arrested emotional development set at around age fifteen to twenty-four months. This suggests that a narcissist acquires slightly more internal security and structure as a child.

There is a continuum of functionality running through all the Cluster B disorders. For instance, individuals who are histrionic are more able to function in society than narcissists, who in turn fare better than those with borderline personality disorder or antisocial personality disorder. This by no means implies that narcissists function perfectly well, or that being in a personal or professional relationship with them isn't torture. (In fact, a narcissist reading this will no doubt twist this information to prove his superiority.) However, this information may provide a modicum of hope in what seems a hopeless situation.

Cluster B Disorders and Continuum of Functionality:

| Borderline/Anti-Social | Narcissistic | Histrionic |

$\longrightarrow$

Lower Functioning   Higher Functioning

WHEN NARCISSISTS SEEK HELP

The narcissist's false self is so grandiose and his ego so cruel and shaming that the disparity between the false self and the ego's internal self will eventually knock him off his pedestal. Sooner or later, narcissists experience a "grandiosity gap" between their fantastically inflated and unlimited self-image and their actual limited and shameful reality. This is why no one can really please a narcissist; the dissonance between what's coming in from the outside world and how they really feel about themselves is agony. In other words, narcissists demand attention and accolade and yet can't tolerate either. The true dread of a narcissist is that someone will find out what a fraud they are, or worse—that they will drown in their own shame. This is when you'll see a narcissist seek help from a professional.

There are typically two circumstances that compel a narcissist to get help. The first situation is the loss of a primary supply. When a spouse or partner finally has had enough and leaves, a frantic and shameful narcissist will often seek therapy or treatment. Those in a relationship with a narcissist often experience guilt, obligation, and codependency that keep them from taking action or setting boundaries. It's my hope that those in this dilemma will realize that the only way a narcissist will accept help is if he or she is faced with the impending loss of a significant relationship or otherwise suffers the consequences of his or her behavior.

The second scenario occurs when a narcissist meets with some failure, often professionally, where his or her manipulation, charm, and control no longer work. Whether fired from a job, turned down for a promotion, or denied membership in a club, the narcissist may first respond with rage. But rest assured that this is only an initial defensive reaction that comes from a profound sense of shame. Very soon you will see the usually inflated narcissist become acutely hopeless, unhappy, and morose—a condition sometimes labeled as dysphoria. This dysphoria is such a sharp contrast to the narcissist's usual display of grandiosity that it's alarming to those around them. Those who are partnered with a narcissist may react with guilt, remorse, and caretaking behavior; they may even reverse the decisions they've made that would have been empowering and self-protective.

Although there are circumstances under which the narcissist will seek help, the motivation to seek help isn't to get healthier or to be a better parent, partner, or friend. When a narcissist seeks help, she wants the therapist to restore her false sense of grandiosity. This presents a significant roadblock to therapists who must be prepared to deal with the defenses of a narcissistic client.

The Narcissist in Therapy

*"A narcissist isn't in therapy to get better.
A narcissist is in therapy to get you to
participate in his symptoms."*

—JAMES MASTERSON, M.D., ONE OF THE PIONEERS
OF OBJECT RELATIONS THEORY

*T*he narcissist is a wounded individual with a disorganized personality. He may agree to therapy simply to avoid the pain of recurrent narcissistic injury. (Kernberg, 2000) Narcissists come to therapy in the first place to try and alleviate some situation that has triggered intolerable pain. Typically, they do not go to therapy because they want to become better people or to better interact with a loving significant other.

Since the root of narcissistic behavior is shame, a narcissist will trigger the shame of anyone who endeavors to get close to them, including a therapist. For this reason, counselors must be aware of and deal with their own shame when conducting therapy with a narcissist. Also, a narcissist has a need to idealize the therapist and then systematically bring him or her down. This roller-coaster ride can be quite daunting, and it's important to remember that this must occur at some point in therapy: the need to project the "bad parent" on to the therapist is part of the healing process. The following case exemplifies this experience.

Don is a well-dressed businessman who has been in a gay relationship for many years. He's quite closeted and neither his family nor his work colleagues are aware of his relationship. His friendships are nonexistent. Occasionally, Don cruises the bars at night and admits that he has had unprotected sex with younger men. He can't comprehend why his partner finally became fed up with this behavior: "If he's boring me, why shouldn't I be able to otherwise entertain myself in the evenings!" His lover wants to break up with him and Don feels both angry and distressed about this situation.

When he first walked into my office, Don seemed rather shy and quite reluctant to describe his lifestyle. His story slowly started to unfold during the first session and I was aware of the amount of pain he was carrying. The first clue that Don had narcissistic traits occurred when, while speaking to him, I quickly glanced over at the clock to see how much time we had left. Don glared at me and snapped, "You know, Rokelle, if you're so uninterested in what I have to say, I know there are dozens of therapists who'd love to have me as a client!" His acute awareness of any small shift in attention sent off alarm bells in my head.

Despite this, we set up several appointments for which he was always punctual. But he was always insulted when I'd ask him to sit in the waiting room until the previous client exited.

At one session he came in and began talking about a handsome young man who had picked him up the evening before. I was amazed that although he was desperate to salvage his current relationship, he would still continue this same destructive behavior. As I listened to his description of this man, I commented on what a deep sense of self-hatred he must have to need and feel so gratified by these fleeting contacts: "Don, are you saying that for a brief time you forget how freakish and unlovable you feel?"

Don looked incredibly sad and said, "That's right. For just a few moments, I feel that I am important and desirable."

"I bet that when my eyes aren't meeting your gaze during our sessions," I continued, "you feel that same sense of unimportance."

Acknowledging Don's shame and keen sensitivity to shifts in my attention formed a cornerstone of our therapeutic relationship.

Gradually Don spoke more about his feelings of unacceptability. He showed his vulnerability when he spoke about his parents, their self-involved behavior, and how he felt both like a showpiece and insignificant. At the same time, his swelling grandiosity began to emerge in his description of work relationships. He described his colleagues as "small items" and unworthy of his abilities. He felt superior to his bosses, thought they were envious of his talent, and believed that he could run the company better than any of them.

Through the course of our sessions, Don began to exhibit the narcissistic overvaluation/devaluation cycle: for a time, he believed that I was the best therapist in town, that he was so lucky to have found me, and that he was going to recommend me to his well-to-do associates. He wanted to make sure that he was my special client and became incensed when I would politely refuse to meet him for dinner. However, as he improved in acknowledging his shame and ceasing his sexual acting out, his attitude toward me moved between gratitude to hurt and annoyance. In other words, I noted a growing competitiveness alternating with real affection. His idealization of me began to diminish as he noted my mistakes in interpretations, my mispronunciations, and at times, my lack of style.

One session, he sat in his chair staring at my hands. I became self-conscious and asked him if there was something wrong. He sneered at me and said, "Rokelle, how can you walk around like that in public?"

I was aghast. I didn't have a clue what he was referring to and asked what he meant.

"Can't you spend the money to have your nails done once in a while? I honestly would be embarrassed to be seen with you."

I looked at my nails and the paint was, indeed, chipping off. I tried to continue the session sitting on my hands but was so ashamed that I had difficulty concentrating. During the lunch break I ran to the manicurist while calling a colleague of mine for consultation.

In short, Don was working through his defectiveness and his issues with his critical, cold mother through transference. I was up on that pedestal for a period of time, but gradually he had a need to see me as similarly flawed. I asked him the next session why the condition of my fingernails was so important to him. He explained how all he felt was disgust and anger, as if my unkempt nails were a statement of my lack of respect for him. In other words, Don had a need to idealize as well as humiliate me. Gradually, as he was willing to tolerate my imperfections, he became more tolerant of his own.

Transference refers to redirection of a client's feelings for a significant person to a therapist. In Don's case, his emotions toward his mother were unconsciously directed toward me. This is exactly the dynamic that is so injurious to lovers, partners, children, friends, and coworkers. In therapy, the key to success is the ability of the clinician to endure this transference without abandoning the process or overreacting. Needless to say, this is a tall order.

When Don focused on my appearance, I had everything I could do to control myself from saying what I really wanted to say. I was so caught off guard and felt such embarrassment that I wasn't able to refocus the issue back to Don until the next session. Yet, this is the key to change. The narcissist is susceptible to treatment only when his defenses are down. Attacks on the therapist are indications that a narcissist is feeling threatened and needs to devalue the therapist; the underside of this response is raw vulnerability.

As therapists, we must endeavor to remain emotionally neutral. If we become upset or distant, we are probably caught in anger counter transference issues of our own. In addition, directly challenging the narcissist is usually unproductive. As a colleague of mine once remarked, "Challenging a narcissist on his or her behavior is like trying to interact with a bucket of tar. The more you try to get at it, the more you become stuck in it."

The idea in calling attention to a narcissist's behavior is to focus on identifying the vulnerability and gently linking it back to his defenses. If you are successful, a narcissist will be able to take in what you say rather than going into narcissistic posturing. Many psychologists believe that it is working in this way with transference that allows the client to grow and to transform. (Jung, 1969)

I must emphasize here that it isn't the job of any child, partner, or coworker to work with this redirection of emotions. However, I hope this discussion may provide some perspective to those who live or work in close proximity to a narcissist by showing that these reactions have absolutely nothing to do with them.

We know that narcissists hold the delusion that they're at the center of the universe. The longing for admiration and attention coupled with this delusion challenges any of us. When a therapist sets boundaries with a narcissist, the reaction isn't going to be pleasant. Any boundary that has been set will trigger a narcissistic wound; yet these limits are precisely what will allow this person to sit with and process their shame. The following example underscores both the need for boundaries and a narcissist's hypersensitivity to lack of attention.

> Mrs. Harris grew up in a family where she had to perform to get attention and was not loved or appreciated for who she was, only for what she could give her parents. She craves attention and when she doesn't get it, the shame becomes intolerable and it quickly turns into attacks on others. She came to me because she was discharged from a law firm due to the way she was treating her clients. She was an excellent attorney, but the firm was losing business because of her outbursts. This incident left her feeling depressed, ashamed, and furious. Mrs. Harris had just lost a

primary source of narcissistic supply and was experiencing the devastating pain of her narcissistic wound. The following incident occurred just when Mrs. Harris and I had reached a level in our work together where she was beginning to disclose her vulnerability:

Mrs. Harris encountered me at an opera one evening. It was during the intermission and I was standing and talking to a group of friends when she came up to me and wanted to engage both my friends and me in conversation. Her husband was with her, but she'd abandoned him in the crowd and rushed over to me. I excused myself from the group and greeted her, and said that I hoped she was enjoying the wonderful performance. After a couple of minutes, I gently excused myself and went back to chat with my friends. In other words, I acknowledged her, but didn't spend the entire intermission engaging with her. I knew there'd be hell to pay, but putting a boundary between my private life and my client was necessary.

In her next session, Mrs. Harris ranted and raged at me for daring to ignore her by spending my time with others. She was insulted that I didn't introduce her to my friends and asked if I was embarrassed to do so. I explained that to protect her confidentiality, I was bound not to disclose her identity. This wasn't satisfactory to her and she even asked me if I didn't introduce her because of what she was wearing that evening! At one point, she glared at me and said, "Your problem is that you think you're too good for me, don't you."

Because I hadn't attended solely to her and because others in my life had commanded my attention, she was incensed. In her mind, I was supposed to be available to her no matter what the circumstances. As we explored her response, it emerged that she had felt

invisible, insignificant to me, and of no importance—
and these were the exact emotions that she had experienced as a child. She left the opera feeling mortified
and worthless. In other words, she left with her own
feelings of shame, a feeling that she desperately tried
to eliminate. In truth, it was her desperate need for
constant validation of her importance to me that filled
her with humiliation. Rage was a reflexive way of rid-
ding herself of this overwhelming emotion.

Since Mrs. Harris came to me with the presenting problem
of her uncontrollable rage, it may have been technically correct to focus on this issue. She could have attended anger management courses for the rest of her life; but that final step of
working back to underlying shame is the key for narcissists and
is, unfortunately, too often overlooked in treatment.

EMPATHY AND COMPASSION
ARE NOT ENOUGH

*"Many people naively believe that they can
cure the narcissist by flooding him with love, acceptance,
compassion, and empathy. This is not so. The only
time a transformative healing process occurs is when the
narcissist experiences a severe narcissistic injury."*

—SAM VAKNIN, 2007

For therapists, it's difficult to work with narcissists and remain
compassionate. They are demanding, self-righteous, and often
insulting.

However, we know that narcissists have been badly wounded

in their lives and we need to maintain our compassion for them. It's quite evident that the extent of their rage and bullying is the extent of their trauma. However, a therapist can empathize with a wounded, grandiose narcissist for a few decades, and that won't shift their behavior.

An effective style for working with a narcissist is one of firmness combined with gentleness; indeed, the model of what a healthy parent should have been. Many of our clients who are diagnosed in the Cluster B category will show up feeling out of control. For many of these people, starting as the nurturing, empathic, gentle therapist in the beginning doesn't make them feel safer; it leaves them feeling more out of control. When working with a narcissist, a therapist must provide nurture as well as structure; narcissists also need the therapist to be especially clear about the direction of their work.

Providing external structure creates the safety necessary to do deep and vulnerable work with a narcissist. And even though this structure will be resisted with behavior ranging from narcissistic fury to endless rationalizations, therapists must hold these boundaries. What do I mean by external structure? Starting and ending the sessions on time, charging for missed appointments, saying no to meetings, dinners, or other social engagements outside the confines of therapy, and resisting the urge to adjust one's boundaries because of one's compassion or the narcissist's intimidation.

By the way, since intimidation is part of the defensive strategy for narcissists, I wouldn't recommend working with this type of client unless one has supervision. The phrase "It takes a village" comes to mind here. Most of us need support to maintain our equilibrium with challenging clients. If a therapist feels physically intimated by any patient, then practicing self-care is imperative. It's not helpful to our clients or to ourselves to continue to be engaged in a therapeutic process when we feel unsafe.

When a narcissist is wounded, he is at greatest risk of acting out against others. Witnessing this reaction and working through the anger of the underlying shame is of great therapeutic benefit. However, when the narcissist's defenses have let him down and he believes his world is collapsing he is at greatest risk of becoming rageful and even violent, particularly if he has a need to seek revenge. Because of the intensity of the narcissist's emotions, the counselor needs to deal very carefully with this anger and avoid a power struggle. During these episodes, the narcissist will sense this and will most likely use this anger to intimidate. Therefore, it's crucial that anyone working with a narcissist receives supervision, learns to self-soothe, and is willing to refer out if necessary.

UNCOVERING THE PAIN

As shown in the story about Don, narcissists may modify their behavior when they learn to reveal why an incident felt painful and are willing to track back to earlier wounds of rejection, betrayal, and shame. Those insights will need to be articulated by the therapist in a descriptive and nonjudgmental way that says, "Of course, you desire nurturance," or "You must have felt very betrayed." Then, the narcissist can begin to soften the rigidity of his or her defensive stance.

Therapists can actually use narcissistic features of their patients to engage and assess them. To avoid angering the patient, it's important to work with, rather than belittle, the narcissistic ego. A therapist can, for example, address a patient's heightened self-importance and desire for control by saying such things as, "Because you are obviously such an intelligent and sensitive person, I'm sure that, working together, we can get you past your current difficulties."

In a crisis situation, the therapist can assess the patient's defenses and put them to therapeutic use. Take the example of a somatic narcissistic patient who complained about his wife's reaction to his anger.

"Rokelle, my wife called the police on me simply for getting angry at her and throwing a couple of things at the wall."

"What did you throw?"

"I threw two garbage bins filled with trash only to make a point. She refused to empty them and said it was my job."

"Had you been drinking?"

"Perhaps I had a few beers after work."

"Let's come up with a plan so this doesn't happen to you. I would imagine that was really a humiliating experience. If you don't want her to call the police, then it will be in your best interest to stop throwing things at her. Next time this happens, you'll be taken to jail. And by the way, drinking not only makes you angrier but also ruins your physique. There is no amount of exercise that can metabolize large quantities of beer. I know you take pride in how wonderful you look and I'd hate to see you ruin your physique."

Obviously, there may be an addiction problem here that will need to be addressed. But the aforementioned dialogue can be a prelude to opening this topic of discussion.

In short, narcissistic personality traits can be used to provide motivation for therapy. The narcissist may be encouraged to change negative behaviors as a reward for recovery: a better appearance, improved career prospects, or improvements in their romantic and sexual life.

USE GROUP THERAPY

It's difficult to do ongoing one-to-one therapy with a narcissist. Group therapy can be helpful for these patients, but the therapist should, tactfully but firmly, place limits on narcissist's speaking time so that they cannot control the discussion or focus all the attention on themselves. Explaining that members of the group need to share the time, therapists may want to make a contract with patients with narcissistic personality disorder before each session to encourage prosocial behaviors. Some of these behaviors include:

- Limiting speaking time
- Not interrupting other speakers
- Respecting the feelings of others
- Responding to other group members
- Listening objectively to responses and feedback from others
  (NIH, 2006)

COUPLES WITH NARCISSISTIC WOUNDS: DINOSAUR BATTLES AND CAT FIGHTS

Narcissistic couples are often chronically angry at each other. These couples often wait too long to go to therapy or may have tried therapy with someone who did not provide enough structure for them. Therefore, they enter therapy frustrated, hopeless, and often bitter.

It's not uncommon to find in couples one arrogant narcissist and one shy narcissist who has lost his or her voice and uses passive-aggressive tactics to express anger. The tragedy of these couples is that after a very short time they withhold love, warmth, and attention from each other. Ironically, what they complain about most is what they cannot tolerate getting.

For instance, picture a session with a narcissistic wife who has a passive, withholding husband. Each session her complaint is the same: "Rokelle, he doesn't share emotions. He's as cold as ice and he really doesn't know how to connect. I will not continue to be in a relationship with someone who is emotionally impaired." Then, when her husband finally shows vulnerability, her reaction is dismissive, petty, and sarcastic: "There you go whining like a baby. Why don't you grow up? I want a man, not a child."

Instead of continuing to meet with this type of couple together, individual sessions would be more useful. The benefit in meeting with each partner separately is twofold: First, it gives the therapist a chance to explore each patient's vulnerability in regard to his or her partner. Second, even though narcissists lack the ability for empathy or compassion, individual sessions are important for setting up a boundary against brutal sarcasm and reactive anger.

Some of the significant qualities and behaviors you'll see in narcissistic couples include:

1. Rapid escalation of hostility.
2. Intense need for intimacy without the skills to support this need.
3. Lack of self-responsibility.
4. Avoidance and intolerance of vulnerability.
5. Inability or avoidance of seeing the impact they have on each other.
6. Repetitive triggering of trauma in each other without the skills to achieve resolution.
7. Lack of compassion or a feigned performance of empathy.
8. Ongoing search for narcissistic supply as an answer to their problems.
   (Bader, 2004)

ENGAGING A NARCISSISTIC SPOUSE IN THERAPY

A colleague of mine worked with a recovering alcoholic who was married to a man with strong narcissistic traits. This woman was rather new in recovery and wanted to work on her painful relationship issues. She indicated that for her, there would be no sobriety unless there was more peace in her personal life. Granted, it's difficult to work on a relationship unless two willing participants are involved, but her husband refused to join her. He made it perfectly clear that although he would pay for his wife to go, it was his wife's problem and for him, therapy would be a waste of his time. In short what he was communicating was, "If you fix my sick wife, we'll be fine."

Through the course of therapy it became evident that this woman could only go so far in working on her relational issues without the presence of her husband. Her situation was so abusive at home that she was close to relapsing. My colleague was puzzled as to how to bring the husband in without forming a posse. With some research, she found a solution using an approach called *paradoxical intervention*. Basically, the purpose of this technique is to stop a problem behavior by prescribing the problem behavior. The following is the letter she sent to this resistant, narcissistic husband:

Dear Joe,

I'm very impressed with your deep commitment to your marriage and your assurance that everything is as it should be. You are to be commended on your willingness to sacrifice some of your own needs, and your willingness to have your wife work ardently on her development and independence. I also appreciate that you are able to encourage Joyce to present her issues in dealing with your marriage, trusting the accuracy of her perceptions about you and the marriage, without feeling the need to come in and discuss your side.

Since Joyce has informed me that you are paying for the counseling, I thought that you would like to know that she is making good progress in her development and clarifying what she wants in the marriage.

Joyce told me that you don't wish to join our sessions and I respect your stand and the firmness with which you adhere to it. Your continued sacrifice in not coming has been very helpful.

Of course, whenever you feel that she has made sufficient individual progress, you're welcome to join us.

As you can imagine, Joe found the letter very unsettling. It dawned on him that he couldn't monitor what his wife was saying about him, and he felt threatened by the fact that she really might be getting healthier. The very next day he called the therapist and explained that as long as his wife had made progress, his participation wasn't going to be a problem for

him. The following week, the therapist found Joe and his wife
in the waiting room. Joe was doting over his wife, holding her
hand, and smiling sweetly—behavior that he used only in the
presence of others.

Clearly, relationship problems are never one-sided. It would
be a mistake to blame all the issues in a relationship on one
partner. Even though a relationship with a narcissist is painful,
the spouse of a narcissist must face certain questions:

- What factors allow him or her to remain in an abusive
  relationship?
- What keeps him or her from voicing their truth and
  setting boundaries?
- What is the family history that taught him or her to
  become resigned to suffering?
- Where did he or she learn that they had the power to
  change or fix another human being?
- What is he or she willing to do in the future and what
  kind of support do they need?

Threatened with the loss of a primary supply, a narcissist
may choose to modify his behavior. (The operative word here
is "choose.") Is this done out of love, remorse, or compassion?
Probably none of the above. Still, it is possible that a couple
can coexist with boundaries in place and more realistic expectations established.

I must add a caveat: if couples therapy concentrates primarily on helping, for example, Joe and his wife communicate
more effectively, nothing much has been accomplished. Even
teaching good conflict resolution skills won't be enough to
help salvage this relationship. For a narcissist, finding the vulnerability under the rage and grandiosity is key, as well as
learning to self-soothe without causing destruction. For a
spouse, the work involves learning how to self-validate, self-

soothe, and maintain boundaries; acknowledging that if he or she doesn't set boundaries they will be consumed; and delving into the reasons for the spouse's high tolerance for abuse.

MEDICATION

Narcissists will generally balk at the use of medication. Since they believe they are above the rest of humanity, resorting to medication is an admission that something is wrong. Many are fearful of becoming one of the masses and losing their uniqueness with medication. Since a narcissist must dramatize his or her life to feel special, one might hear the following rationalization: "I am not like anyone else in the world and medication affects me differently." Contrast that to narcissists who claim to have discovered new and revolutionary ways of using medication: "I'm experimenting with this medication to benefit humanity." Suffice it to say that if they are prescribed medication, many narcissists will likely refuse it, or use it in ways that are not productive.

Narcissistic personality disorder cannot be effectively treated with medication alone. The underlying disorder is managed by long-term psychodynamic or cognitive-behavioral therapies. However, the symptoms associated with narcissism, such as depression, obsessive-compulsive disorder (OCD), pathological lying, paranoia, and angry outbursts are sometimes treated with selective serotonin reuptake inhibitor (SSRI) medications such as fluoxetine/Prozac. It's possible, however, that if SSRIs are not used as prescribed, adverse effects may lead to agitation that exacerbates the rage attacks that are typical of a narcissist. Not enough is known about the biochemistry of NPD but there is research that indicates success in using heterocyclics, MAOs, and mood stabilizers, such as lithium, that don't have the extent of unfavorable side effects that SSRIs do. (Lowen, 2004; Vaknin, 2007)

Constructing a non-defensive self through therapy or treatment is not short-term work for the narcissistic client. There are many obstacles to overcome and still the prognosis for significant change is minimal. It's of utmost importance that those in relationship with a narcissist delve into their own issues, practice self-care and boundaries, and learn how to deal with the emotional abuse that exists in relationship with a narcissist. There is a danger for those in relationship with narcissists to avoid working on their own issues. Many times through the years I've heard spouses of narcissists express that the source of their pain is centered on the behavior of their husband or wife: "So what does that have to do with me?" There is a belief that if their partner goes to therapy or treatment, romance will return and life will be happy again. Unfortunately this is a pipe dream and far from the truth.

PART

4

SURVIVING A NARCISSISTIC RELATIONSHIP: BREAKING THE SPELL AND COMING TO LIFE

Trapped in a Narcissistic Relationship: Why You Can't Help Yourself

There is a painful double bind that exists when you're in relationship with a narcissist. Many feel trapped in a dilemma of feeling powerless to leave, yet unable to stay. The narcissist's ploy is to provide just enough love and attention to lure you in, followed by large doses of mistreatment or abuse. This lethal combination is called intermittent reinforcement, which is an extremely addictive psychological bond. There are good reasons why those involved with narcissists feel as if they're sleepwalking through some bad horror movie and feel crazy much of the time. The following provides some explanation about why it's so difficult to extricate yourself from this type of relationship as well as tools to cope with the narcissist in your life.

FEARS OF ABANDONMENT

Abandonment fears are not unfounded in relationship with a narcissist. Although a narcissist desperately needs to be in relationship, the exposed shame and painful wounds that are triggered around abandonment become intolerable. In addition, narcissists sense that their partner will inevitably see how inadequate they are and leave for someone else. Rather than wait for that reality, they'd rather control the inevitability and leave first.

For a narcissist, abandonment is triggered by two illusions: that exiting the relationship will stop his anguish, and that somewhere out there is the ideal partner who really knows how special he is. What ensues is a painful, repetitive cycle. The narcissist leaves. Then he often returns, expressing feigned remorse and promising more effort and commitment to change. The abandoned partner feels a renewed hope for a better future, only to be set up for abandonment again.

Naturally, partners of a narcissist want to know how to prevent this cycle. The answer is that you cannot. Once a narcissist has reached this point of escaping the pain by exiting the relationship, the prognosis isn't particularly hopeful. The problem for those in relationship with narcissistic partners is that you spend so much of your time either thinking about leaving, or trying to avoid being abandoned, that you lose track of who you are. This erosion of spirit happens day by day until you don't even recognize yourself. The first step to your own healing is introspection. Turn your focus inward and contemplate the reality of your situation.

In order to face the reality of why you've stayed in an empty relationship, it may be time to face the fears that have been buried deep within you. Abandonment fear alerts us that our hearts need to be healed if we're to grow in our capacity to give and receive love.

Many people suffer painful relationships because they fear being alone. They'd rather give themselves away than face an empty house or apartment. They're willing to accept leftover attention, the status of mistress, or rage and abuse rather than face their deeper fears of abandonment or aloneness. This is a fear most humans face no matter what kind of family background exists. For those who were emotionally or physically abandoned as children, however, this fear plays a major part in their motivation to stay connected to someone despite the cost.

Are you tired of walking on land mines and using all your energy just trying to avoid issue after issue? Do you wonder what happened to that person within you who used to feel confident, free, and joyful? Are you fretting about the next time you'll make a mistake and set your partner off on a rampage or days of silence? Are there so many topics that are forbidden to discuss that you find yourself desperately searching for things to talk about—ironically, to the one who is supposed to be closest to you? Is fear of abandonment eroding your spirit? Are you in the hideous position of not being able to stay in this relationship, yet not being able to leave? If so, it may be time to look at your abandonment issues. (Skerritt, 2004)

Can you imagine what it might be like to speak your truth with dignity, to express your opinion without repercussions? Wouldn't it be wonderful to feel the delight of give and take rather than, "I'll give and you take." It is our birthright to be free, to express our opinion, and to live without fear. But remember this caveat: honesty without sensitivity is called brutality. With the gift of freedom comes the inherent responsibility of respecting the boundaries of others. This is something that a true narcissist cannot do. However, through long-term therapy a narcissist can modify his or her behavior.

Dr. David Berenson, a physician and family therapist, has a quote I'll never forget: "If you don't come to terms with your fear of abandonment, you will never be able to act with abandon." (Berenson, 1998) How true this is! If we don't face our abandonment fears, we'll never be free. We'll always be walking on tiptoe, making sure that no one leaves us. We'll squeeze the life out of our relationships as well as ourselves. In this way we attempt to control others so that we don't have to confront our darkest fears of abandonment.

THE PARALYSIS OF BLAME

Blaming has always been one of the top ten tools for propaganda and can keep a victim paralyzed with fear. In wartime or periods of financial hardship, there is always a scapegoat. The vicious treatment of particular racial groups was used to unify communities against a common enemy. In fact, years ago Russian President Gorbachev said something curious to President Reagan. He said, "Mr. President, we're going to do something terrible to the United States. We're going to take the enemy away."

As long as there is someone to blame for our hardships, we can direct our anger outward. If there is no enemy, then anger and shame implodes. It's been hypothesized that the rise in violent crime and abuse in our culture began to seriously increase after the detente with Russia. Perhaps you can see that when it comes to a narcissist, the need for an enemy, or a few enemies, is crucial to keeping shame at bay.

Narcissists are adept in manipulating and brainwashing people close to them so that the victims will take on the guilt. They blame the victim unjustly for causing them distress as a way of avoiding taking personal responsibility. It's a slick, convenient way to demoralize a subject, while making the narcissist look superior. For narcissists, this particular mind game is honed to an art form.

The narcissist is adept at mind games. The term "mind game" can be used for any strategy or tactic where mental manipulation or intimidation of another person is a goal. One mind game occurs when a narcissist engages you in a battle by blaming you, coercing you to attack until the narcissist finally ends up in the victim role. Then it is your opportunity to feel sorry for this victim and begin to rescue him from his despair. The Karpman Triangle shows this dynamic that is so common in narcissistic relationships. (Karpman, 1974)

KARPMAN TRIANGLE

Persecutor: "Look Susie, Mom is so lazy she can't even make dinner on time"

Persecutor: "Don't you dare talk to me that way in front of the kids!"

Victim: "I guess I can't do anything right."

Rescuer: "Well I know you've had a hard day a work."

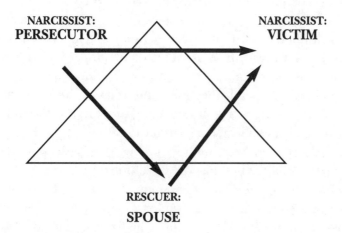

NARCISSIST: **PERSECUTOR**

NARCISSIST: **VICTIM**

RESCUER: **SPOUSE**

In working with narcissists, I find that the only motivation for them to cease the blame-and-attack games is the potential loss of supply, which is always looming over them. It's possible for narcissists to see how this blaming defensiveness takes away from the things they long for most—love and acceptance. If this narcissist ever chooses to get help, the challenge to a therapist would be to find the deep hurt underneath the blame and to redirect each attack back to the narcissist's underlying vulnerability.

But I Love Him

Loving a narcissist can be extremely addictive and leaving him very difficult. Say whatever you'd like about narcissistic relationships, they are not boring. Of course, the conflict, sarcasm, and loneliness get old, but narcissists stir up drama in every relationship.

When I hear partners of narcissists say how they love their spouses, I must delve into their interpretation of that love. It's not that I disbelieve them, it's that in a narcissistic relationship there's a profound confusion between intimacy and intensity. For example, if the relationship contains a high level of fear, betrayal, abandonment threats, passionate reconciliations, or sexualized affection, then one is referring more to intensity than to intimacy. After all, attachment often deepens with terror and this intensity is so absorbing and addictive that it can feel just as powerful as true intimacy. The danger then becomes that although they know the relationship is causing them harm and that they should leave, they are not psychologically or neurochemically prepared to do this.

Dr. Robert Sternberg, author of *The New Psychology of Love* (Sternberg, 2006) writes that love is painfully paradoxical; it's the only thing that matters and it's absolutely not enough to make a relationship work. This realization for those who are in love with narcissists is a bitter pill to swallow. The torture of loving someone who is hurtful to us, added to intense feelings of obligation and self-doubt, keeps us locked in situations no one else would endure. Suffice it to say that waiting like a puppy for a sign of loving behavior from a narcissist is a setup for starvation.

Generally, our disappointment and hurt in another is rooted in unrealistic or thwarted expectations. (Brown, 1999) If, after repeated difficult and cruel behaviors, you say things like, "I'm sure this will never happen again," or "If I just work a little more (give more, do more, be more), I'm sure things will change," then you are clearly blinded by the nostalgia of earlier days when your narcissistic partner was loving, romantic, and caring. Perhaps those memories are sacrosanct to you because that's all you have left to cling to. Today, you're spending your life trying to please a partner who cannot be pleased.

The problem is, even though we might be excruciatingly aware that a partner is harmful to us, the feelings of love continues to draw us back to this person. This dilemma produces such shame and helplessness that it not only diminishes our joy, but what's worse, damages our integrity. This awareness keeps us isolated, afraid, and in a perpetual state of despair. We become so hungry for scraps of affection that we're willing to sacrifice our soul, our friends, our jobs, and sometimes even our children. We become constricted and singularly focused in the presence of our narcissistic partner; each action we take and each word we speak becomes measured.

This is the oppression of loving a narcissist. Clinging to your love for a narcissist as a rationalization to avoid setting boundaries, staying safe, and practicing self-care is a huge barrier to healing. Love doesn't mean putting up with someone's destructive behavior, and if this is something you recognize in your relationship(s), then the first step is to have compassion for yourself. Only then can you begin to reverse the one-way valve of attention and admiration that's sapping your life's energy.

Asking some individuals who have been ravaged by their relationships to have compassion for themselves is like telling the homeless to "just buy a house." It makes sense why compassion for self is so difficult in a narcissistic relationship.

When you're involved with someone who is unable to show empathy, your capacity for self-empathy becomes lost. (See cycle of isolation, depression, page 185.) Starved for understanding, you have become brainwashed; your internal voices of inadequacy and self-doubt drown out any possibility of your having self-compassion. When empathy isn't displayed in a relationship, you feel as if you're unlovable, undeserving, and at fault. Not because of some action that causes you to feel guilty, but because you feel you are defective or flawed in some essential way. Gradually, shame begins to sit where your soul used to be. And shame cannot exist with self-love. (Kaufman, 1992)

COMPASSION VERSUS SELF-PITY

*"Whining is anger coming
through a very tiny opening."*

—MARY LEE ZAWADSKI, AUTHOR

There is a difference between compassion for yourself and feeling sorry for yourself. Feeling sorry for yourself is very closely related to feeling anger. In fact, some would say that self-pity is really "anger in a party dress." And while it may feel safer for some people to engage in self-pity rather than anger, rest assured: they are two sides of the same coin.

No one likes the term self-pity, and there may be reasons why this emotion is familiar to you. Perhaps you've inherited a legacy of self-pity or bitterness from your family. If you grew up with a martyr and have taken on his or her posture toward life, then your intense anger at yourself (and later at your partner) has gone unexpressed. Now it comes out in self-deprecation and whining. If a parent consistently played the martyr role in your household, you may have promised yourself that self-pity is something you'll never resort to. However, the early patterning may be engrained and will most likely emerge in your adult life. Whatever its cause, your anger can be expressed in responsible and life-giving ways rather than in passive-aggressive, half-hearted ways. Self-pity connotes victimization and martyrdom, and even though you may indeed feel victimized, this attitude will prevent you from taking action and will inevitably drive people away.

Compassion is a form of nurturing self-love. It's not abusive, manipulative, or angry. Compassion doesn't involve self-pity. Rather, it involves tenderness, mercy, kindness, warmth, and love—in short, everything you've offered up to your narcissistic partner that you've denied yourself. When you practice compassion it's as if you're becoming the loving parent to the part of you that feels wounded, small, and insignificant. In this way, you learn to love yourself into taking action, voicing your truth, and breathing life back into your soul.

In order to move from self-pity to compassion, you must take a serious look at the painful cycle in which you've been living. Many who are in relationship with narcissists today have felt trapped their entire lives. When you finally realize how powerless you've felt with a narcissist and/or with mothers or fathers that were narcissists, your internal despair and anger toward yourself and others is understandable. Although knowing why you've felt these emotions will not bring about solutions, it can clarify your perceptions and reassure you that you're not crazy. The following diagram explains the tragic cycle that may seem familiar to those whose lives have revolved around a narcissist:

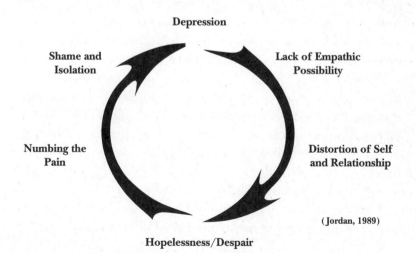

A painful cycle of shame, isolation, and depression occurs when you're in relationship with a narcissistic partner. When, time after time, you receive responses of indifference, injury, or denial of your experience, you gradually begin to dismiss these important aspects of yourself. You agonizingly come to the painful realization that there is no possibility for connection or empathy in your primary relationship. Because most of us can't consciously accept this fact, many face a horrible dilemma. On some painful level you know that this situation isn't going to change, yet you continue to hide integral parts of your being in order to keep the relationship going. Systematically, you conceal your feelings, your opinions, your successes, your failures, and your truth. After a time, you don't recognize the person you've become. You turn into a creature so irrelevant that it seems impossible that you ever had a voice at all.

As humans, we have a basic need to make sense of our lives and make some order out of chaos. When we can't make sense of the way we are being treated, we wind up distorting our view of ourselves and our relationships. Instead of directly addressing the pain, we try harder to please the narcissist; in fact, the anxiety over trying to "do it right" is so overwhelming, that we can't possibly be present for our family, our friends, or even ourselves. Ironically, because of this anxiety, we are more prone to making mistakes, mixing up our words, and feeling as if we're small and inept—thus manifesting a self-fulfilling prophecy.

Since we are under the spell of a narcissist, we assume that we are the cause of our partner's unhappiness. If we were just smarter, more attractive, sexy, or worthy, things would be different. In other words, since we are brainwashed into thinking the problems are about *our* deficiencies, we believe we can fix the relationship by fixing ourselves. This is a desperate attempt to control the uncontrollable.

When we feel incapable of making the situation better, we go into hiding. Out of hopelessness and despair, we become convinced that any opportunity for a meaningful interaction with our beloved is impossible and we lose the ability to reach out. The helplessness of the situation leads to an internal sense of humiliation and we begin to distrust our ability to connect with others. It's then that we begin isolating ourselves from the support of friends and family. Ironically, it's the very tendency to pull away from others to protect ourselves that most locks us into shame. (Jordan, 1989)

By the way, the powerful purpose of shaming people is to silence them. The modus operandi of a narcissist is to stop anyone who gets in the way of his illusion of power and grandiosity. His tactics are actually rooted in shamelessness and a lack of conscience. Shaming is a sinister mode of oppression, in many ways more effective than physical tyranny. Indeed, shame has always been a potent use of dominance to subdue expressions of the truth. In narcissistic relationships, the self-perpetuating cycle of shame leads to isolation and then to a profound and deep depression where you feel immobilized to take action, to get help, or to save yourself.

This cycle applies to ongoing relationships with narcissists and, to a great degree, to living or working with people with borderline, antisocial, or histrionic personality disorders.

There is one important factor that needs to be considered regarding shame, hopelessness, and depression. Perhaps these emotions are haunting, repetitive, and familiar echoes from your family of origin, where as a child you felt trapped in a similar cycle. If this is true, then chances are you feel like a child in your adult relationship with absolutely no alternatives available to you. When this occurs it's difficult to stand up for yourself and feel empowered because you're seeing the present through the eyes of your past. Delving into your history and recovering your lost inner child may be the next important step. The following chapters provide strategies that will be helpful in removing yourself from this cycle in order to find a way of being in a relationship that is life giving.

Strategies for Maintaining Your Sanity with a Narcissist

*T*he most important first step toward healing and growth for a potential codependent in relationship with a narcissist is to recognize the deeper picture of the narcissistic disorder. Once you realize that there's nothing you can do to fix your partner and that you've been under his or her spell, developing healthy boundaries will allow you to maintain your equilibrium in the midst of all the insanity.

BOUNDARIES: THE KEY TO CONFIDENCE, CALM, AND SELF-CONTROL

Healthy boundaries are a statement of the dignity you have for yourself and for others. Any relationship will fail without boundaries. Since a narcissist has no boundaries and could not care less about your boundaries, all interactions you have with them have the potential of becoming hideous. Narcissists assume that others are so mesmerized by their beauty, intelligence, and charm that the need to respect limits isn't even in their consciousness. Entitlement, after all, is the name of their game. This means the responsibility for setting and maintaining boundaries is yours. If you are waiting until your partner, child, or coworker "gets it," you'll probably be waiting until the next life.

There are two purposes for boundaries: protection and containment. Protection means that what you value—your sanity, your privacy, your physical and emotional well-being—you will protect. It means that if someone is threatening to attack you in any manner, you'll find a way to either put a halt to that behavior or leave the scene. Those with narcissistic personality disorder (NPD) will trigger anxiety, fear, and anger in the ones that are closest to them. If you reside, work, or otherwise have a relationship with a narcissist, you must find a way to either tune them out or guard yourself from assault. This is easier said than done.

Containment is our ability to control our emotions *until* we've had the chance to think about what we're doing. It's the type of boundary that a narcissist will not acknowledge and feels too entitled to practice. However, just because your coworker or partner spews their emotions everywhere and causes havoc doesn't mean that you need to behave in the same way. Practicing containment means you are able to rise above the turmoil and find your sanity. (Lerner, 1995)

You might be saying to yourself, "I've tried setting boundaries and it doesn't make any difference!" If you mean that the behavior of your partner or coworker doesn't seem to change, you're right. If you're saying that establishing boundaries didn't work because he or she got angry or agreed to treat you with respect and then didn't, ask yourself why you would expect anything else from a narcissist?

Despite this, it's possible that his or her behavior will change in relationship to you. Why? Because narcissists are in such dread of losing their supply that when someone close to them sets limits and then follows through, their fear of abandonment is one of the few factors that will compel them to change. Granted, these changes aren't done in the spirit of altruism or compassion, but it's possible you will see a decrease in the bullying, rage, and insults.

In an ideal world, we would set our limits with others and they would reply, "Isn't it wonderful that you're saying, 'that's enough' to me! I'm so proud of you for saying *no*!" That will rarely, if ever, happen with anyone, let alone a narcissist. Remember, like the victims of vampires, you've been under a trance—perhaps for many years. If you're waiting for a narcissist to give you affirmation, tenderness, or otherwise take care of you when you set your limits, then you are absolutely correct in thinking that it's not going to make any difference. However, if you set your boundaries with absolutely no expectation, you will be halfway home. It becomes a matter of validating and reassuring yourself. It's knowing deep in your soul that if you don't do this, you will die a very slow and painful emotional death.

Many individuals with narcissistic partners, coworkers, or children have lost their voices. In other words, they gave up on speaking their truth after a short time in these relationships. I realize that speaking up after years of zipping your lips is not easy. But the payoff for reclaiming your voice is an increased feeling of self-respect and empowerment. (Bader & Pearson, 2003)

In order to set boundaries with a narcissist, you must prepare adequately. Practice exactly what you want to say with the right demeanor and the right tone, and then look for the right timing. In other words, if your partner comes home ranting and raving about work, it's self-sabotage to broach the subject of boundaries. Sometimes when we have something difficult to do, we feel such anxiety that we just want to get it over with as soon as possible. Practice self-care by waiting for the moment when you have the most chance of being heard.

The most important thing to remember is that you must do what you say you're going to do in order to be taken seriously. The inability to follow through with our commitments to ourselves often keeps us feeling hopeless. If you say that you'll leave the room, the house, or the relationship if a particular behavior continues, and then don't do it, why would anyone take you seriously? What's worse is that this lack of follow-through damages your own soul and destroys what little confidence you may have.

Why We Don't Set Boundaries with Narcissists

When we're intimidated, many of us feel like small children. We feel disempowered, we lose our voice, and we want to run and hide. And when we feel small, we tend to speak with the fear of a child and not with the grace and strength of a man or a woman. I call this dynamic "shrinking." It happens to all of us at one time or another. However, when you're feeling like a child and trying to speak your truth to a narcissist, you may as well kiss your dignity good-bye. This, by the way, is exactly what narcissists want. They want you to submit your power to them. They want you to quake in your shoes at the thought of a confrontation with them. So be advised, it's not safe to let your inner child lead the dance in your relationship with a narcissist. Think about it this way: would you let a nine-year-old drive your car? Of course not. But a similar thing happens when we can't "grow ourselves up" and find our inner strength.

There are four tools you can use to move from feeling like a child to becoming an empowered adult. These tools do not have to be used in this order presented, nor do you have to use all four. Implementing at least two of these rules can make a significant difference in your ability to voice your truth and maintain your dignity:

1. Set a limit.
2. Make a request.
3. Take an action.
4. Name the emotion you're experiencing.

Set a limit, make a request, take an action, and name the emotion: sounds simple, right? Then why is it so challenging to implement? The problem lies not just in remembering to do this, but actually moving into action when we're anxious, afraid, hurt, or vulnerable. When we're in the midst of an argument, some of us would rather finish it to its hideous conclusion then practice what we know we should do. A number of us are overtaken with shame, and the accompanying despair paralyzes us. For most of us, behaving differently is out of our comfort zones. Even though we realize that what we're doing doesn't work, even though we know that it's stripping us of our dignity, there's a kind of solace in the old, albeit sick, behavior. Truly, the most intimate relationship we form is not with another human being; it's with our comfort zone. A therapist named Rich Simon puts it this way: "For me, change is not an adventure. It's a scary ordeal to be endured if necessary, but avoided if at all possible." (Simon, 2007)

To understand why these four statements work so powerfully, it's helpful to understand what happens to the brain when we're faced with conflict. There are three distinct and separate cerebral units in the human brain:

- **Prefrontal Cortex:** The prefrontal cortex is involved in making decisions, making plans, and taking action. It has a significant restraining role over impulses and actions.
- **Amygdala:** If you remember only one word about the amygdala, that word would be *fear*. The amygdala is the primary center for identification of danger and

self-preservation responses, such as fight, flee, freeze, or faint. The amygdala is the center responsible for the lurch you feel in your stomach when you turn around in a dark alley and notice someone following you.

• **Limbic:** The limbic system is primarily responsible for our emotional life—mood, motivation, pain, and pleasure.

Someone told me once that "Life is God's way of seeing if we can take a joke." It's a truly cosmic joke that there's not more connection between the cortical analytical brain and the emotional/limbic brain. For example, have you ever tried to talk yourself out of being in love? When the emotional brain is active, the cortical brain doesn't have as much influence as we'd like. For instance, how well do people think when they're anxious, afraid, or angry? When we're frozen in our fear or anxiety, we can't think clearly or articulate well. Thus, if we can practice setting limits, making requests, taking an action, and naming the emotion, we can begin to activate our "adult" brain. Only then can we move from reactivity to integrity.

Incidentally, the purpose of naming your emotion when you're upset is to calm your brain's response to danger. According to Dr. Mathew Lieberman of UCLA, "if you name your emotions, you can tame them." Brain scans show that putting negative emotions into words calms the brain's emotion center. "In the same way you hit the brake when you see a yellow light, when you put feelings into words, you seem to be hitting the brakes on your emotional responses.(Lieberman, 2007) The following is an example of one man who implemented the tools of setting a limit, taking an action, and making a request to finally speak his truth to a narcissistic wife.

John was a client I'd been seeing for about six months. He'd had enough of his wife's raging and her critical treatment of him. He found that he dreaded going home each day and resented that he'd let the situation get this awful. He spent his life with Diane feeling imprisoned with no chance of pardon. Each day as he started the drive home from work, he vowed that this would be the day that he'd finally stand up to Diane and be clear about his limits. Instead, when he got in the door he felt afraid and hopeless. If Diane was irritated about something, he knew he would be blamed and would tiptoe around the house in order to keep the peace. If Diane was relatively pleasant, he tiptoed around the house anyway, hoping not to make waves. John was trapped in his own fear and allowed Diane to determine night after night what kind of evening he was going to have

At work, John was assertive, successful, and well-respected by his clients. This discrepancy between work and home eroded John's self-esteem, as day after day, he'd give his power over to his wife. He was so humiliated about his situation that he never invited friends or colleagues to his home.

One evening when John's car was stalled, his coworker, Art, offered him a ride home. John accepted and when they reached his house, John didn't see Diane's car in the driveway and invited his colleague in for a drink. To his shock, Diane was talking on the phone and pacing back and forth in a wild frenzy. He invited Art to sit down and tried to make conversation amidst the ranting and raving of his wife. In a few minutes, Diane hung up the phone and shrieked, "I asked you to pick up milk and you forgot. You know, John, you really are a useless man!"

Diane marched into the living room with a scowl and was preparing to say more when she noticed Art sitting in the chair. Her demeanor changed miraculously. She walked over to John, put her arm around him, and said, "Darling, I didn't know we had company." She walked up to Art and warmly greeted him and invited him to stay for dinner. Art said he had a commitment, made his good-byes, and left.

Mortified and angry, John summoned the courage to confront his wife that evening. When he started addressing her treatment of him, Diane came over, stuck her finger in his face, and let the venom spill. Instead of backing down, John firmly requested that she get her finger out of his face. After a few minutes Diane turned to him and yelled, "Don't you dare tell me what to do!"

At that moment, John felt an all-too-familiar fear creep into his consciousness. He was starting to lose his train of thought when he remembered what I had suggested he do when he felt fear.

"I'm going to use the bathroom and we'll continue this in a few minutes," he told Diane.

John left and closed the door to the bathroom. He first acknowledged his emotional state: "I'm feeling anxious and afraid." He looked at himself in the mirror, took a couple of deep breaths, and gave himself the affirmation that he'd been practicing for months: "You can do this. There's nothing she can do to you that you haven't already experienced. It's time to take charge of your life."

During the course of the conversation with Diane, John had to leave the room twice. Each time, he returned feeling slightly more empowered and was finally able to say the things that needed to be said for a long time. Diane responded with vitriol and anger. John responded by excusing himself, going to his study, shutting the door, and listening to music on his "sound-canceling" headphones.

When John came in for his next appointment, his demeanor was different. Instead of a hopeless, despairing tone of voice, he appeared more upbeat and stronger. He described the encounter with Diane and the aftermath of her rage at him. It was clear that she hadn't changed, but John's behavior had changed with Diane. In other words, he found his self-respect again.

"Something is different, Rokelle," he said. "I feel as if I can take care of myself and stop acting like a victim begging for her approval. I even talked to Art at work and resisted the urge to apologize for my wife. Her behavior is her problem."

John felt a sense of pride that he was able to stand up to his wife without cowering or backing down. He realized that he could only do that by developing his boundaries and "growing himself up." He loves Diane, but he realizes that love is not enough. If she continues to disrespect him, he may have to leave the relationship. He realizes that the lesson he has to learn from this is that he deserves respect, that he doesn't have to remain a victim, and that it's up to him to take action by setting and maintaining boundaries.

He was able to safeguard his integrity by making a request (don't point your finger at me), naming his emotion (I feel anxious and afraid), and taking an action (excusing himself and leaving the room when he felt intimidated). These types of behaviors literally influence the movement of neurotransmitters in our brains from the limbic, emotional brain to the cerebral cortex. In this way, we can *think* about what we're *feeling*.

Practical Magic: Putting Boundaries into Action

Most of us realize that if we feel ourselves "shrinking" yet continue to speak, our words will undoubtedly come across as weak and unconvincing. If this happens, it's crucial to excuse yourself immediately. If you're able to do this, your narcissistic partner will be startled, upset, and eventually anxious that you're gaining fortitude.

Here are some convenient exit statements:

- I need to use the bathroom.
- I forgot to make a phone call.
- I need a glass of water.
- I just forgot that I left some papers in the car.
- I'd prefer to discuss this later. How about tomorrow evening?

Or, if you're feeling bolder:

- "When you speak to me in that tone, I cannot continue. I'm going to leave the room. Let me know when you're ready to listen without yelling."
- "I'm trying to understand, but I'm feeling attacked. Could you tell me what you don't like without sounding harsh? I'm fine with you saying, 'I didn't like it when you let me know about our appointment three days before it, when you knew for weeks.' That's easier for me to hear than when you say: 'You are an arrogant woman.'"

When you approach a narcissist with your boundary requests, I suggest that you start with this statement: "There are some things I need to say to you, and while I'm speaking, I request that you don't interrupt me. *Can you do that?*" If the answer is anything but *yes*, then simply state, "When you're ready to listen without interrupting, please let me know," and then leave the room. You don't have to have an argument or be engaged in a dialogue about this. Remember, the more you get snagged into a discussion, the more you lose your power.

Keep in mind that very few of us had any guidance in developing healthy boundaries and no one will establish their limits perfectly. However, if you're not willing to follow through with what you say you will do, then it's better not to say anything at all. Instead, practice in front of the mirror, practice with friends, and build up your emotional muscles. When the time comes that you feel ready to share your boundaries, then summon your dignity and speak with the poise of an adult. The following example of protection boundaries may be helpful:

- "If you bully me either when we're alone or in public, I will ask you to stop. And if you continue, I'll leave the room."
- "When you rage at me, I feel frightened. My request is that you contain your anger and let me know what you want in a calm way. If you continue to rage at me, I'll leave the house (or the relationship)."
- "If you insult me (by calling me names, picking on me, and so forth), I'll ask you to stop. If you continue this behavior, I'll leave the room. If it happens again, I'll leave the relationship."
- "When you embarrass me in public, I feel mortified and hurt. If you do this again, I will leave the gathering immediately. If it happens a second time, I will not go out with you in public."

Work-Related Boundaries

Setting boundaries at work is complicated. Many of us can't stand the way we're treated by narcissistic employers or clients; yet we can't afford to lose our jobs. As we discussed in chapter 8, you're the one who will have to discern the emotional price you're willing to pay by remaining in the employ of a narcissist. In the meantime, here are some suggested dialogues that both appease this type of employer but set limits in a gentler way:

- "I value your feedback, and it's important to me. I'm wondering if you could give me your feedback privately so that I can really listen to what you have to say."
- "When you insult me during our meetings, I really feel blindsided. I want to learn from you because you have so much to teach me. My request is that you stop calling me names so I can really listen to you without becoming distracted. If this happens at future meetings, I'll have to leave the room temporarily, but be assured, I will return."
- "When you ask me to run errands for you, like picking up your dry cleaning, I get really behind in my work. If you can't do it, I'll be glad to help you out sometimes, but you're paying me too much to do this on a regular basis and I don't want to waste your money."

CONTAINMENT:
FROM REACTIVITY TO INTEGRITY

When a narcissist is being insulting, on a rampage, or simply behaving horribly, it's difficult to avoid reacting. When we're being attacked, it's not as if we can stand there looking up a

particular passage in our books or rummagi⌐
handouts for the right thing to say or do. Wha╵ ╴╴
is that we shoot from the hip and respond in the same old
ways—and get the same old results.

When attacked, we need to quell our reactions. It's not that
we have to remain stoic, but if a narcissist knows he or she is
having the desired effect, chances are the behavior will be
repeated. When you're in the midst of fiery narcissistic fumes,
it will be necessary to both protect yourself from the onslaught
and contain yourself so you don't become an offender. The
following nondefensive actions/statements by Dr. Brian
Walker are invaluable when you're on the receiving end of
someone's strong emotion:

> Remain silent, nod your head, and give the impression
> you're listening. Or make statements such as these:
>
> - "Oh?" or "Hmmm . . ."
> - "Maybe so." or "Could be."
> - "That's a very interesting opinion."
> - "I want to think about what you're saying."
> - "What are you trying to tell me/ask for?"
> - "Why is that so important to you?"
>   (Walker, 2007; Smith, 1985)

Do these actions/statements resolve the issues you're facing? Of course not, but they give you time to think, breath, and
calm down without emotionally reacting or "shrinking." To
make some order out of your chaos, I suggest memorizing the
statements and using them when you're facing a narcissistic
tantrum.

If you want to have even more impact with a narcissist, make
your statement with a friendly tone of voice and a gentle
facial expression. Speak clearly, calmly, and confidently. Avoid

allowing your voice to rise at the end of a sentence, particularly if you're stating what you want and need. Doing so undermines what you are saying. Amazingly, if you relax the muscles in your face and especially around your eyes when you talk, your attitude will become softer with less effort. Using these techniques, the narcissist may still blow strong, harsh wind, but your sails won't be up to catch that wind. The outcome will be that you won't be bashed into the rocks trying to recover from yet another emotional shipwreck.

If someone doesn't respect your boundaries, you will inevitably have to leave them in order to salvage your integrity. If you've spoken your truth and set your bottom line for the relationship to continue, and your partner breaks this boundary and continues the behavior, then you have your answer. The answer is either that this relationship is not of value to this person or that the state of his or her emotional or mental health prevents him or her from honoring this boundary. Regardless of the reason, when we keep moving our boundary lines, the price we pay is shame, anger, grief, and the loss of self-esteem.

Having said this, it's not uncommon to reach the point of letting go, only to have the narcissist deliver the most compelling and unbelievable seduction story. Desperate about losing his primary supply, you will most likely witness a performance of warmth and caring that is of Oscar quality. This is when you will need the courage to confront your own internal longing for the seduction to be true. (Carnes, 1997)

It's important to prepare yourself before you talk to a narcissist. The Confrontations, Concerns, and Boundaries worksheets on the following page is a guide for determining your boundaries, your emotions, and your requests. This blank worksheet is followed by a sample worksheet to help you get started. Be advised, that when you make requests of narcissists, they will do whatever is in their power to resist answering

Confrontations, Concerns, and Boundaries Worksheet

When you: _____
Like the time: _____

                     _____
I feel (felt):   _____
My request is: _____

                     _____

When you: _____
Like the time: _____

                     _____
I feel (felt):   _____
My request is: _____

                     _____

When you: _____
Like the time: _____

                     _____
I feel (felt):   _____
My request is: _____

                     _____

Boundaries—Protection

If you: _____
I will take care   _____
of myself by: _____
Instead of: _____

If you: _____

I will take care _____

of myself by: _____

Instead of: _____

If you: _____

I will take care _____

of myself by: _____

Instead of: _____

Boundaries—Containment

When I feel: _____

I will take care _____

of myself by: _____

Instead of: _____

When I feel: _____

I will take care _____

of myself by: _____

Instead of: _____

_____

When I feel: _____

I will take care _____

of myself by: _____

Instead of: _____

_____

SAMPLE
CONFRONTATIONS, CONCERNS, AND BOUNDARIES WORKSHEET

When you:	Insult me in public
Like the time:	Last week when you told me I was stupid at a dinner party
I feel (felt):	Hurt, ashamed, angry
My request is:	That you no longer put me down in public. Will you do that?

When you:	Rage at me when I disagree with you
Like the time:	Last night at the dinner table when we were discussing the weather
I feel (felt):	Hopeless, afraid, angry, and ashamed
My request is:	That you either respond to me calmly or tell me you'd rather not talk

When you:	Don't let me leave the room and interrogate me
Like the time:	I went out with my girlfriends for lunch last week
I feel (felt):	Angry, humiliated, anxious, and suffocated
My request is:	That you never block my exit again

Boundaries—Protection

If you:	Continue to insult me in public
I will take care of myself by:	Leaving the room immediately
Instead of:	Sitting there and feeling embarrassed

If you:	Rage at me when I disagree with you
I will take care of myself by:	Tuning you out. If I can't do this, I'll leave the room
Instead of:	Engaging in a heated argument about inconsequential subjects

If you:	Block my entrance or exit to a room
I will take care of myself by:	Standing still, giving you pat answers and then leaving the house. If this continues, I'll call the police and leave the relationship
Instead of:	Resigning myself to suffering and remaining a victim in my own house

Boundaries—Containment

When I feel:	Ashamed
I will take care of myself by:	Stepping out to calm down and growing myself up
Instead of:	Feeling sorry for myself and enduring your criticism of me

When I feel:	Afraid
I will take care of myself by:	Going to my friends' house, setting limits with you, or leaving the room to calm down
Instead of:	Remaining helpless or entering into fights with you

When I feel:	Hopeless
I will take care of myself by:	Calling my therapist, spending time with my friends

you. They will blame, manipulate, rage, change the subject, be seductive, and so forth. It's your job to keep this person on track. You deserve an answer and there are three possible, suitable answers to your requests: "Yes, I will," "No, I won't," or "I'll think about that and get back to you." (If this is the answer, you have the right to know when the request will be answered.)

You may be asking yourself, why should I bother making requests? The reasons why we make requests are twofold. First of all, you're much more likely to get your needs met if they're stated in the form of a request instead of a demand or anxious whining. Secondly, just because our narcissistic partners or employers behave in an obnoxious manner, it doesn't mean that we have to adopt their style.

ONCE A VICTIM, TWICE A VOLUNTEER

Even though this statement may be harsh, it's something that the prey of narcissistic vampires have to consider. Not being a victim or a volunteer comes down to making a choice: either take action or remain in a miserable cycle of suffering. The choice is yours. When you resist doing what you know is in your own best interest, you remain a victim. I'm not saying that making the choice for yourself is easy, or that those who won't or can't do it are to be judged. I'm suggesting that if you're in this situation, you've abdicated your power and your choices. It's as if you're under a spell and the only one that can break this spell is you.

If you've become resigned to suffering, I would remind you that we're not saints, and we're not supposed to be saints. Not only that, but there's also a legacy of suffering that some parents inadvertently pass down to their children. I'm reminded of a cartoon of a mother with a huge cross on her back, staring at her children who are surrounding her. She's bent over from the weight of this cross and her children are looking up at her with concern in their eyes. The caption is "Someday this will be yours." (Giersch, 1989)

In relationship with a narcissist, there's a difference between being a victim and being a survivor. A victim is someone who's still in a state of denial about being emotionally, physically, sexually, or spiritually abused. A victim has been contaminated by the narcissist's curse and sincerely believes that if he or she could just be smarter, prettier, thinner, more muscular, or more talented, their spouse wouldn't treat them so hideously.

A survivor is someone who is awakening from the trance of being a narcissist's supply. They are beginning to grasp that they are not responsible for their partner's vicious cruelty, raging, lies, or unreasonable jealousy. They are people who are aware that the narcissistic dynamic is not their fault, which is immensely relieving and an important step toward healing. However, let me pose a question: how many of you are content with just surviving for most of your life? For most of us, the idea of spending our lives in survival mode is like a jail sentence with no parole. Consider then that the next step is a transformation from survival to thriving.

Thriving is beyond survival in that we take responsibility for our own healing. We no longer tolerate abuse in any form. We defend ourselves from further mistreatment by setting boundaries and following through with commitments we've made to ourselves. The movement from victimization to empowerment/thriving looks like this:

Victim: "I don't believe I'm being mistreated." "It's my own fault that she treats me that way."
Survivor: "I am not responsible for the reactions of the narcissist in my life."
Thriving: "I am not responsible for the way I've been

treated. But I am responsible for the solution, the resolution, and my protection, so it never happens again."

I must add that if you are a partner of a narcissist, you're coping with grueling circumstances that you did not create. It's important that you avoid shaming yourself and sinking into despair. In other words, obsessing about how stupid and how damaged you may be sets you up for further ridicule and abuse.

The following poem speaks beautifully to this struggle and has been an inspiration to many who have lost themselves in their relationships:

Love After Love

The time will come
when, with elation
you will greet yourself arriving
at your own door, in your own mirror,
and each will smile at the other's welcome,
and say, sit here. Eat.
You will love again the stranger who was your self.
Give wine. Give bread. Give back your heart
to itself, to the stranger who has loved you
all your life, whom you ignored
for another, who knows you by heart.
Take down the love letters from the bookshelf,
the photographs, the desperate notes,
peel your own image from the mirror.
Sit. Feast on your life.

—*Derek Walcott*

*B*uilding Your
Psychological and Spiritual
Immune System

*I*f you're reading this book, you have the desire to change your life. If you feel helpless to alter your situation, it's not because you don't have the strength to do it; rather, it's because your emotional muscles have become atrophied from lack of use or misuse. Let's use the metaphor of the body: if you're exposed to the flu and you happen to be stressed, tired, and generally run down, your immune system is weakened and you'll probably become ill. Similarly, if you've lived or worked with a narcissist, it makes perfect sense that you're feeling emotionally depleted, weary, and hopeless.

To avoid becoming emotionally ill, it's crucial that you begin to build up your emotional immunity through setting boundaries, practicing self-care, and getting the proper support. Only then can you summon the strength to take a different direction in your life.

So many lose their way in painful relationships due to the misuse of their energy and attention. And the price we pay is enormous. We no longer know what our purpose is in life. It's difficult to remain true to our purpose when perspective is gone. At the end of your life, you want to know that your life has made a difference and that you have left a positive legacy. Instead of winding up bitter and regretful, it's time to enhance your psychological and spiritual well-being. There are three timeless questions that will help you reclaim your life. Ask yourself these questions on a daily basis:

1. Who am I?
2. What am I meant to do here?
3. What am I trying to do with my life?

We are all given a purpose to fulfill in this life. We're all given gifts that we're supposed to nurture and then give to others. At the same time, we must be discerning about the recipients of our gifts. Sadly, many of us keep bestowing gifts on those who either can't receive or who keep taking and taking until we're consumed. Some of us are so drained that we don't even know what we want anymore—except that we want our narcissistic partner to change.

Our immunity becomes destroyed when we get invested in trying to control the uncontrollable. To shift your focus ask yourself: "What does my heart long for?" or "What do I want?" Some of you may not know the answers to these questions. If this is true, it means that you've thrown your needs in the garbage. Like the sick joke of the drowning codependent, who with her last breath saw someone else's life pass before her eyes, if you don't know what you want, it's not that you won't get anything. You'll just keep getting what you don't want. One way to get back on your path is to think about your priorities.

PRIORITIES

A "priority triangle" is filled out from the bottom space to the top. The *bottom* space represents your most *important* priority; the second to the bottom space is your second most important priority, and so on. Instead of writing down what you think your priorities should be, take a moment to reflect on the last year of your life. Whatever has taken the most mental and emotional time and energy would go on the bottom rung. Then consider what area of your life has taken the second highest amount of time and energy.

The priority triangle below is from a woman who has lived with a narcissist for eleven years:

PRIORITY TRIANGLE

QUESTION: What's taken the most time and
energy over the last year?
(Completed by a spouse of a narcissist)

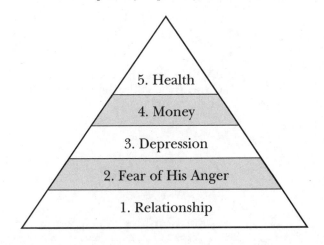

5. Health

4. Money

3. Depression

2. Fear of His Anger

1. Relationship

Now, draw your own triangle and do your best to suspend your judgments. Your judgments can sabotage your intentions, and this is for your eyes only. You may share it with a close friend or a therapist, but I suggest you resist sharing this with the narcissist in your life. The idea is to take a long and hard look at the way you've been living.

No one can tell you what your priorities should be; it's none of their business. If an area of your life is in crisis, of course it will be your top priority. But as in the example of the woman who lives with a narcissist, her painful relationship has remained her top priority for over a decade—to the exclusion of her emotional and physical well-being. She has given up on all but one of her dreams: "Some day my husband will look around and I'll be gone. He'll miss me so much that he'll do anything to get me back." To date, she remains with him and hasn't been without him for more than a couple days before returning home.

The triangle below is an example of living a balanced life. When we're feeling in balance, then our actions are congruent with our deepest desires. This is not to say that the following have to be your priorities, but they are a good check for all of us, particularly those of us who've been focusing our energies on just being able to survive another day with a narcissist.

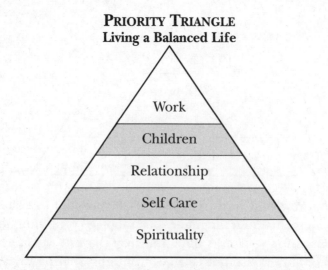

PRIORITY TRIANGLE
Living a Balanced Life

Work

Children

Relationship

Self Care

Spirituality

When I first saw this priority triangle I thought to myself, "Oh great. Another 'New Age' spin on our problems!" Listing spirituality as the most important priority doesn't mean that we can spiritualize our problems and they'll disappear. But how many of you have felt helpless, despairing, and profoundly alone in your relationship? Christina Groff, therapist and author, would call this a spiritual emergency. It's called a spiritual emergency because it's a crisis that contains within it the seeds of transformation. Spirituality is a connection to something in the universe greater than us. If you've already spent significant time with someone who already behaves as if he or she is omniscient and omnipresent, then your notion of a higher power becomes warped. (Grof, 1994)

Dr. Abraham Twersky, psychiatrist, rabbi and addiction therapist, has a wonderful quote about spirituality: "Religion draws people who don't want to go to hell. Spirituality draws people who have already been there." (Twersky, 2000) This means that when people face pain in their lives, that pain will either break them apart or break them open. For some who feel as if they've been sucked dry by a narcissistic vampire, it may be time to nurture their faith. The seed of spirituality is gratitude. Practicing a ritual of gratitude each day diminishes fear and gives birth to trust. In this way we learn to walk a spiritual path with practical feet.

Practicing self-care is the second highest priority you can give yourself. Putting yourself ahead of your relationships is tantamount to serenity and peace. Remember the directions we hear on the airplane: "Put your own oxygen mask on first before you help someone else." When we focus on our own care, then we have more to bring to our relationships. Even though this is perfectly logical, those for whom this book is written have usually been unable or unwilling to take action on this.

Relationships are the third priority. Doesn't it makes sense that we need to take care of our emotional, physical, and spiritual health if we are to share ourselves with another? For partners of narcissists, relationships have been the sole focus of life. Obsessing, agonizing, and strategizing have taken precedence over our health, our family and our joy.

You'll notice that children are further up on the priority triangle. As women, most of us were taught that children always
come first. Unfortunately, always putting children first is often
an escape from dealing with a narcissistic partner. Focusing on
our children can be a convenient escape when we don't feel safe
in our primary relationships. In addition, research has shown
that it isn't good for children to be the top priority in a household. We have a nation filled with children who feel entitled,
can't really manage for themselves, and can't endure uncomfortable emotions because everything is taken care of for them.

Work is the fifth priority in this triangle. In our culture, we
are pushed and prodded to make work our top priority. A colleague of mine who leads tours to Tibet once told me, "In
Tibet, they bathe once a year and pray every day." It's quite the
opposite in our culture. Obviously we need to make a living
and hopefully we're doing something that adds meaning to
our lives. However, work can be another convenient escape to
avoid a painful relationship. If we're not careful, we wind up
sacrificing our health, our children, and our serenity just to
avoid going home to the tirades of a narcissistic partner.

Taking Back Your Life:
The Thirteen Steps to Sanity

The following suggestions will help you get the focus off the
narcissist in your life. If you follow through with these initiatives,
you'll gradually feel your strength, your courage, and your dignity return. If you practice these techniques daily, you'll feel a
difference within a very short time. However, consistency is the
key. Remember to be gentle yet firm with yourself. Every cell in
your body is going to want to stay in the old paradigm of inac-

tion and resignation. Tell a close friend or therapist what you're going to be doing. That way, when you feel stuck, you can call on them for encouragement:

1. Set up a strategy.
2. Set clear boundaries.
3. Practice self-soothing.
4. Learn to walk away.
5. Practice detachment.
6. Find a support community.
7. Abdicate taking responsibility for the narcissist.
8. Don't take a narcissist's behavior personally.
9. Don't expect understanding or empathy from a narcissist.
10. Never use NPD as a weapon.
11. Focus on the reality and not the potential.
12. Get reality checks from those you trust.
13. Stop making excuses and denying the severity of the problem. (Adapted from Hotchkiss, 2003)

Set Up a Strategy

It is important to have some kind of strategy during times when your narcissistic partner is either on a rampage or emotionally withholding care, love, and affection. For instance, if you become ill and need caretaking, make sure there is a friend or relative who can come to your aid. Also, if you find yourself the target of a narcissistic tirade, devise a strategy to protect yourself. Is there a neighbor, friend, or relative where you can temporarily go until your partner is calmer? If you have children, think about how you can protect them from overhearing the arguments.

It would be advisable to let your partner know of these plans. Instead of just turning on your heels and disappearing, excuse yourself and let him/her know that you'll be leaving and will return when he can talk about the issue in a calmer manner. If you become ill, there's no need to discuss what support you have lined up. This is simply practicing self-care that doesn't depend upon whether or not a self-indulged partner will come through for you. If he does, it's wonderful; if he doesn't, then you won't be left stranded.

Other elements of creating a plan involve your daily activities. As an example, plan at least one entire afternoon with those who are uplifting and positive. It's important to be surrounded by supportive, heart-centered people who make you feel safe and secure. It would be advisable to get yourself on some kind of schedule that feeds your physical, emotional, and spiritual well-being. Exercise, leisurely walks, and support groups are among the few options that partners of narcissists will need to build their immunity. Take care of yourself so that you're not left to a narcissist's mercy at the beginning of every weekend. For example, go and do something fun either with yourself, with your kids, or with friends.

If the narcissist is in your work environment, see if any adjustments can be made that allow you to work closer with those who give you energy. If not, at least plan ways in which you can limit your contact with those who sap your energy.

Set Clear Boundaries

When you're in a relationship with a narcissist, it's crucial to set limits in terms of where and how long you will interact with him or her.

Be polite, but be firm. When approaching a narcissist, remember this: the difference between being mean and setting boundaries is attitude. Be prepared: it's probable you will be called selfish, unreasonable, or much worse. Why? Because you are no longer allowing the narcissist to treat you poorly, manipulate you, or force you to rescue him or her from his or her own pain. Decide what behaviors are and are not acceptable. When a situation arises, clearly and patiently explain your boundary and your feelings about why you set this boundary. When your boundaries are tested, defend them. You have a right to have your boundaries respected. Say no, kindly but firmly. The bottom line is that if someone continuously refuses to respect your boundaries, it's time to think seriously about the high price you pay for remaining in that relationship.

Practice Self-Soothing

Learning how to calm down is the key to setting boundaries. It's practically impossible to get clarity on what you need when you're hurt and angry. This is typically when we wind up feeling small and diminished and the consequence is that what comes out of our mouths sounds like the words of a small child rather than those of an empowered adult. (See page 192 on "Why We Don't Set Boundaries with Narcissists.") During these times we long for someone to comfort and reassure us. Sadly, this is not something you're going to receive from a narcissist.

All of us are challenged to find ways in which we can stay calm in the face of conflict. To depend upon others to comfort us when we're upset leads to a symbiotic dependency where we'll be perpetually disappointed. For those who either live or work with narcissists, it's time to find your particular method to achieve composure. Many know how to do this and yet forget to implement these tools during crucial moments. This is where prioritizing self-care and having the discipline to follow through is a life-saving gift. The following chart will help you discern different strategies for soothing. I suggest you read this sample chart, come up with some self-soothing strategies of your own, and develop a practice of reviewing your strategies first thing in the morning. If you take this practice seriously, you will no longer remain a victim in your personal or professional relationships.

Sample Self-Soothing Chart

	At Home	At Work
WITH A NARCISSIST	Excuse yourself and call a friend for support.	Nod your head as if you're listening and take deep breaths until you feel calmer.
	Excuse yourself and say that you'll return when he/she is calmer.	Surround yourself with an imaginary plastic bubble and watch the words bounce off of you.
	While in conversation, envision her/him as a scruffy, messy toddler having a tantrum.	In your mind's eye, shrink them down to the size of a mouse and listen to them screech.
	Trust your intuition that always informs you when a battle is about to start. Then, take yourself away, go for coffee, and read a book.	Memorize and use the non-defensive statements when you're in the midst of a narcissistic tantrum. Practice saying them in a confident manner.
	If your partner treats you rudely around others, simply get up and leave the room. No apologies necessary.	If the narcissist at work is embarrassing you, stay calm and feign as if you're writing something down until the maelstrom passes.
BY YOURSELF	Attend a weekly support group like CODA, Al-Anon or some spiritual/religious fellowship.	Get weekly support from a mentor or someone you trust to help maintain your sanity.
	Move your body daily to release tension: yoga, dance, exercise, brisk walk.	Before you come home at the end of the day, take the time to gentle down before you walk in the door.
	Participate in some pursuit that brings you joy and relief from stress: reading, art, writing, jogging.	Use an affirmation daily: "Not one more day am I allowing ____ to decide what kind of day I'm going to have."
	Take a class in something that really interests you. It is a life-saving tool to refocus on yourself.	If you spend much of your time in fear or dread, ask yourself if the fear is more about the present or the past.
	Avoid self-pity by making a daily gratitude list.	Resist the urge to use your spouse as a "target" for your fear/anger.

When a narcissist has harshly impacted us, taking utes for ourselves is necessary in order to bring us back to some equilibrium. By calming the mind, we can regain our focus. There are many ways to calm down even for those who can't sit and meditate. Here are a couple of exercises that you can do either standing still or slowly walking outside:

Close your eyes, focus on your breathing, and gently relax your body. If you can keep the focus on deep breathing, that's a good way to quickly reconnect with your life force.

Find a place outside or inside to sit. It doesn't matter where, but if you're trying to detoxify from a narcissistic "dump," it's preferable to leave the house temporarily. When you've found a quiet place, focus on your senses. Start with five sensations in each category and then go on to four sensations, then three, until you feel calmer. For the best results it's advisable to go through this list twice.

Start by focusing on:

- Five things you can see
- Five things you can hear
- Five things you can touch
- Five things you can smell
- Five thing you can taste

This exercise is particularly helpful if you suffer from anxiety and can't stop from obsessing or ruminating. Focusing on your senses is an extraordinary method of putting yourself in the present moment, relieving stress, and strengthening your emotional boundaries.

Learn to Walk Away

One of the most useful tools you can use to defend yourself from a narcissistic onslaught is to walk away. If you feel overwhelmed don't hesitate to politely excuse yourself from a nasty conversation. Move at least twenty feet from the person, outside the range of his or her energy field. "I have to go to the bathroom" is a foolproof line. Narcissists are oblivious to how their energy impacts others. When you feel trapped, physically removing yourself is a sure, quick solution. When we get engaged in battle, we are not only reduced in the eyes of a narcissist, but we lose our self-respect and become diminished in our own eyes as well.

When you're with a narcissist who you can't get away from, visualize a protective shield surrounding every inch of you. You can even visualize words and toxic venom bouncing off this shield while you smile politely and act as if you're listening. This is particularly efficient for narcissists at work when you're in their presence for eight hours a day.

Practice Detachment

This is a concept that always sounds good in theory; the practice of detachment, however, is a transformative skill. And, it's particularly difficult because narcissists work hard to build up a feeling of obligation, hoping it will keep us locked in despite the way they mistreat us.

The word "detachment" doesn't mean that you turn cold and no longer care about another. Rather it means that you learn to care from a place of perspective. When you are able to detach, you have the ability to maintain an emotional bond of love, concern, and even deep caring, without emotional devastation, rescuing, or controlling.

There are many reasons that keep us from detaching from the madness, which are exemplified in these statements:

- "If I stop being involved, what will he do without me?"
- "Being detached seems so cold and aloof. I can't be that way when I love and care for a person."
- "If I let go of this relationship too soon, he might change and be like the fantasy or dream I want him to be."
- "No matter how bad my loved one has hurt and abused me, I must be forgiving and continue to extend my hand in help and support."
- "My partner is really damaged and can't help herself. I know that deep down inside she really loves me and I'm the only one who can help her."

If any of the above sounds familiar, it's possible that you're not willing to let the person you love take personal responsibility for his or her own actions. Perhaps you've been deluded into thinking that you have the power to change him or her. But taking marriage vows doesn't mean that your job description entails being a therapist or a martyr.

The following is an excerpt from an anonymous poem that explains the process of letting go:

> To let go doesn't mean to stop caring. It means I can't do it for someone else.
> To let go is not to cut myself off. It's the realization I can't control another.
> To let go is not to enable, but to allow learning from natural consequences.
> To let go is to admit powerlessness, which means the outcome is not in my hands.
> To let go is not to care for, but to care about.
> To let go is not to judge, but to allow another to be a human being.

*To let go is not to be in the middle arranging the outcome, but
   to allow others to affect their own destinies.*
*To let go is not to be protective. It's to permit another to
   face reality.*
To let go is not to deny, but to accept.
*To let go is not to nag, scold, or argue, but instead to search out
   my own shortcomings and correct them.*
*To let go is not to criticize and regulate anybody, but to try to
   become what I dream I can be.*
*To let go is not to regret the past, but to grow and live for
   the future.*
To let go is to fear less and love myself more.

Find a Support Community

Groups like Al-Anon, Codependents Anonymous, or religious groups are available when you're feeling isolated and need to get started with your healing. When we summon our courage and raise our heads in a support group, we are embraced with faith. People whom we don't (yet) know assure us with perfect confidence that we are good people. And their faith in us can be the catalyst that gets us out of a terribly stuck place. This kind of help can also come from healthy, supportive family, or even from therapy. However, therapy alone can take years to accomplish what we need to do. Therapy combined with support is the catalyst for change.

Research shows that it's not self-esteem that contributes to psychological well-being, but rather how connected we are to others. (Eisenberger & Lieberman, 2005) Lack of confidence is a measure of how much we've isolated ourselves. Just like a fuel gauge provides a readout of the amount of gas in a car to prevent an empty tank, self-esteem provides a readout of how connected we are to others. The more isolated we are, the more we feel depleted, shameful, depressed, and hopeless.

Abdicate Taking Responsibility for the Narcissist

Our narcissistic spouses must be first and foremost responsible for themselves. We allow ourselves to be trapped in the idea that we must be responsible for what our spouses do and what might happen to them. The truth is that we can never be responsible for another adult, nor should we try to be. Everyone is responsible for his or her own feelings. If you feel responsible, you're under the spell of a narcissist. For some of us, this is a false belief that we were raised to accept as truth. However, whether you're an employee or a partner of a narcissist, this was never in your job description.

Don't Take a Narcissist's Behavior Personally

"What you think of me is none of my business.'

TERRY COLE WHITAKER

Narcissists have a mental illness that is, to date, incurable. It's a tall order to suggest that you must not take the verbal tirades and attacks of your narcissistic partner, employer, or child personally. However, this is exactly what you must attempt to do in order for sanity and reason to return to your life. Taking back your power means that when a narcissist speaks to you, it will be in your own best interest to be mindful of the mental illness that plagues them.

To keep from being devastated by narcissists, it helps to understand that they generally detest themselves. This self-hatred then becomes projected on to the people closest to them. Even though it's tragic that they've been raised with these narcissistic wounds, in adulthood they have the choice to get help and they have the choice to notice how people around them are responding to their bullying and rage.

Ironically, this won't happen until the people around them stand up for themselves and stop wilting in the face of these outrageous attacks, or when the narcissist is faced with the loss of a primary supply.

In order to withstand the barrage of insults and vitriol, look at the narcissist as if he or she were a two-year-old having a tantrum. Visualize him jumping up and down, throwing himself on the floor, and yelling at his mother to have his own way. In your mind's eye, shrink him or her down to the size of a toddler. Remember that narcissists became emotionally stunted around eighteen months of age and this is the "child" that shows up in an adult body when he or she doesn't get his or her way.

If you must communicate with a narcissist on a regular basis, resist the urge to be defensive. Defensiveness only adds fuel to the fire and you'll leave each conversation feeling diminished and hopeless. Remember that the narcissist's statements are personal opinions and are not necessarily valid. Instead of responding to a narcissist with the same critical and blaming demeanor, use the nondefensive answers listed on page 201. For example, "I'll think about that" or "That's an interesting viewpoint" are superb statements that build a valuable shield of safety around you.

Reading affirmations, doing self-talk, and reminding yourself of your worth will be essential for survival. If the attacks escalate and you're feeling victimized, then remove yourself from the situation. You are powerless to change a narcissist, but you do have the responsibility to protect yourself. And if you have children, it will be of utmost importance to remove them from the scene.

As a wife of a narcissist so graphically put it, "When a bird poops on you, it isn't your fault. You just happened to be where gravity caused the deposit to drop. Wipe it off and keep on living. Do the same in response to other people's behavior.

Instead of taking the behavior personally, and then getting angry, consider the source and then walk the other way."

Don't Expect Understanding or Empathy from a Narcissist

> *"Expecting empathy from a narcissist is like running to the hardware store for raisins."*
>
> —CHRIS RINGER, THERAPIST

A narcissist is emotionally incapable of empathy or remorse. They may give a stellar performance, but there is no substance to their words. In fact, they can be so convincing that they truly care about your pain, many of us can be seduced in a heartbeat. Just as in the legend of vampires, a narcissist will do whatever he or she has to do in order to secure their prey. Tragically, those in relationship with a narcissist are so hungry and desperate for love and compassion that they keep setting themselves up to be wounded.

It's unsafe to show vulnerability or express emotional or even physical need with a narcissist. Even though it's our birthright to have our basic needs met, it's perilous to expect this self-absorbed person to fulfill these needs. If by chance your narcissistic partner does meet your requirements, believe me, you will pay a high price. Many of you realize this, and yet you can't seem to stop yourself from "running to the hardware store for raisins." And every time you get rebuffed, hurt, and disappointed, you vow never to depend on this person again.

Never Use NPD as a Weapon

No matter how frustrated and enraged you become, resist the urge to call your partner a narcissist. First of all, it will only trigger more abuse and his reaction may be quite volatile. Secondly, it's not your job to diagnose your partners, coworkers, friends, or children. No one likes their faults and weaknesses pointed out to them. And even though this probably happens to you quite often, I suggest you curb this kind of attack, primarily because it's unproductive, revengeful, and in some cases, perilous. A competent, empathic therapist must make a diagnosis of narcissistic personality disorder in the privacy of his or her office.

Focus on the Reality and not the Potential

*"I live in another dimension.
I have a summer home in reality."*

What if you knew that your partner or spouse was not going to seek help and that these narcissistic characteristics were not going to disappear? While it would be wonderful for a narcissistic spouse to change, it's not likely to occur. Unless you see this person for who he or she is, you will live in a cycle of suffering and become perpetually more hurt and bitter. Unfortunately, dwelling on "if only" and "some day" keeps you from taking care of yourself and, in some cases, your children.

The Buddhists have a poignant way of describing this. This tradition teaches that although one's fabricated reality can be uncomfortable and even painful, anything outside this reality is called "suffering." Philosophers like Spinoza talked about suffering as the compulsive desire to persist in achieving an unattainable goal. When we spend our time chasing after a fantasy, we're more likely to act in ways that are not in our own best interest. Controlling, pleading, martyring, and not being present for our own lives are just some of the prices we pay. The remedy to this is not simplistic, but it's simple: we must let go of the desire to change our narcissistic spouse or see her or him as anything but seriously and perhaps permanently impaired.

Get Reality Checks from Those You Trust

Being in close daily proximity to a narcissist can cause you to lose your perspective. For this reason, it's crucial to be able to check out your point of view with those you trust. Preferably, these are people that don't have a relationship with the narcissist in your life but do have impeccable boundaries. A therapist is someone who can give you reality checks as well as affirm your sanity. However, when a therapist isn't available, we need to be able to call on a trusted friend to give us clarity. Having someone with whom you can confide is critical for moving forward in your life and bringing you out of isolation and shame.

Stop Making Excuses and Denying the Severity of the Problem

One gift you can give yourself is to start believing that your partner, employer, or child has a severe problem. In part, acceptance will help you defend against a narcissistic onslaught. Acknowledgment of your partner as a narcissist means you begin to take their insults and tantrums as part of their illness and not a statement of fact. In order to stop being perpetually wounded, you must accept that the narcissist is an irrational, unhealthy, and toxic influence in your life. If you begin to label him or her honestly for what he or she truly is, not only will you stop minimizing the negative impact, you'll be able to stand in the face of a narcissistic attack and maintain your sanity. (Brown, 1999)

A LIST OF DO'S AND DON'TS FOR PARTNERS OF NARCISSISTS

Don't ask your partner to change or complain to him about how badly he treats you. The narcissist is probably not even listening to your complaint, but getting ready to go into attack mode. Save yourself the trouble of another battle.

Do concentrate on building your own self-respect and strengthening your own emotional immune system. Validate your perceptions of healthy versus unhealthy sharing.

Don't press a narcissist to share feelings. If you encourage or prod a narcissist to share feelings, it will not end well. Either you'll be in for an attack, or you'll be there for hours listening to a lecture.

Do manage your own anxiety. Usually we badger others because of our uneasiness. If you depend on a narcissist to soothe your anxiety, you're setting yourself up to be used and humiliated. Instead, tune in to your emotions. and when you feel desperate to connect, call a friend, take a walk, or listen to some music until the anxiety abates.

Don't try and please your partner so that he or she will notice and appreciate you. Trying to appease your partner only places you in a hideous double bind. A narcissist wants you to bend over backwards for him or her and yet will see you as pathetic and weak. There's no way to please a narcissist, so conserve your energy.

Do what pleases you! Ask yourself each day, "What do I need today?" "What will bring me the most serenity and well-being?"

Don't engage or retaliate with verbal abuse

Do decide to act on your own highest values, no matter what your spouse does. Don't be dragged down into the muck of your narcissistic partner.

Don't be seduced by the narcissist's promise for future change. Narcissists have no intention of fulfilling promises unless there's something in it for them. Typically, a partner of a narcissist is so hungry for love that he would rather believe anything than see the harsh reality of his situation.

Do bring forward your adult realism and take the narcissist's promises with a grain of salt. Remember how many times your heart leapt at assurances that things would change, just to be disappointed and heartbroken once again? In the case of a narcissistic partner, words are cheap and it's action that counts.

Don't allow yourself to be financially dependent upon a narcissist. It is dangerous and puts you and your children at risk.

Do strive to be financially independent of the narcissist. Begin to develop your own financial resources. The key word here is "begin." It doesn't have to happen immediately; the idea is to be thinking about how you can best be assured of some financial safety. At the very least, find out what assets you both have and how they are being used. You have every right to know this information. If you have to do this without the knowledge of your partner, then find an accountant who can assist you.

Don't allow your fantasies about your narcissistic partner to ruin your life. Fantasy helps us get through very difficult and painful situations, but it can also be dangerous. If you can't see your partner for who she is but what you want her to become, you will continue to set yourself up for profound disappointment, shame, and unending emotional and/or physical abuse.

Do remember that potential isn't enough to save a relationship. Can you envision yourself years from now, still turning somersaults and hoping for crumbs of attention and kindness? You cannot get affection, warmth, or understanding from *potential.* You can't get your emotional or physical needs met from the person he *might* become someday.

Don't medicate yourself with food, alcohol, drugs, or other compulsive behaviors in order to delay grieving. When you face the realities of your relationship, it may throw you into grief and despair. Rather than facing these emotions, many set out on a path of self-destruction.

Do allow yourself to grieve the death of your dreams. If you're someone who loved deeply, then your heart is shattered and will take some time to heal. By allowing yourself to grieve without medicating your emotions, you'll come face to face with the loss of your fantasies and dreams. The most profound loss is the dream of the partner with whom you could feel loved, cherished, and safe.

Don't beat yourself up for choosing a narcissistic partner. Did you wake up one morning and think to yourself,

Today I'm going to find some narcissist to love and be miserable. Haven't you been beaten up enough? By continuing to be harsh with yourself, you remain loyal to your narcissistic partner and the emotional battering that was given to you.

Do recognize that you're not insane; your situation is toxic. Perhaps it's time to differentiate your sick relationship from being a sick person. Chances are, you're having normal reactions to living in a dysfunctional situation. The most profound lessons we learn in our lives are through our relationships; this doesn't make us damaged. It makes us human.

Don't fall into the trap of denying your role in the relationship.

Do learn the powerful lessons that relationships teaches you.

To avoid making the same mistakes, take your own behavior into account as well as your partner's. For instance, you may recognize that there may have been reasons you chose this person or stayed too long. You may learn that your boundaries were weak and needed to be strengthened, or that you continually deferred to your partner. This perspective will help you move forward in your life.

WAITING FOR SELF-ESTEEM

Most of us assume that high self-esteem is essential in order to move forward in our lives, that in order to take action on difficult emotional situations, we first need to raise our confidence. Although I concur that self-esteem and confidence are vital to well-being, if most of us waited for high self-esteem to take action in our lives, we might be too old to enjoy it.

Popular psychology has really confused us regarding self-esteem:

- Before you have an intimate relationship with another, you'd better have good self-esteem and know who you are.
- Don't take action on important decisions in your life until you build your confidence.

I don't disagree that relationships work better if both people have a solid sense of self, or that it's better to take action on important decisions when you're feeling a sense of confidence. However, if we all waited to know ourselves before we had intimate relationships, we'd have happier unions, but they'd probably take place in a nursing home. If we waited to make decisions until we had high self-esteem, we'd stay stuck on issues for years. Self-respect doesn't magically descend from the heavens or spring up one day while we're having breakfast. Self-esteem doesn't come from reading books or going to therapy. Self-esteem develops when we're willing to do the right thing even when the choices are difficult. Self-worth comes from making decisions about what needs to be done and then taking action.

When we eventually say what has to be said to our narcissistic partner, it's not done in safety and security, and it's not done because we believe in ourselves. We begin to take action because we get to a point where our fears of attack and rejection pale in the face of losing our soul. This is the leap of faith that builds our emotional strength, self-esteem, and self-respect. The more we can speak our truth with dignity, the less we'll have to tiptoe on eggshells and live in a state of perpetual anxiety.

Wouldn't it be great if we could receive empathy and validation from our partner as we bravely and respectfully speak our truth? How lovely it would be to hear, "You're right darling. I really have treated you badly and I'm so very sorry." Those who live or work in close proximity to narcissists are probably saying to themselves, "There's no way that would ever happen," and they would be absolutely correct. In truth, the challenge for every human being is to rely on their own resources when empathy and affirmation are not available.

When we summon our courage and we self-disclose, we know that our partners will not like it. To expect anything else is a set-up for pain. A renowned therapist, Murray Bowen, puts it this way: "If you start changing and people around aren't complaining, if they're not telling you to go back the other way, they liked you better before, then you probably aren't accomplishing anything!" (Bowen, 1990)

The Light at the End of the Dark Tunnel

*N*arcissists can turn the sanest individuals into victims. You may recall that your partner's behavior at the beginning of the relationship was charming, generous, and caring. Not only that, but the emotional abuse probably didn't appear until a lasting commitment was made. That's when everything changed for the worse. There are no simple ways to extricate ourselves once the knot is tied, particularly if we have children to care for. Plus, many of us still remember the dazzling courtship and we're waiting until that person shows up again. This "now you see it, now you don't phenomenon" is the most addictive attachment there is. It keeps us hooked to potential and paralyzes us.

No doubt you've felt that something is desperately wrong in your life. At the same time, you've felt so trapped by the narcissistic spell that you've felt unable to free yourself. The important factors to recognize are that your situation is unhealthy, that there are no simple options to make it better, and that you have some difficult choices to make. That doesn't define you as sick, but it does define you as a person who is being challenged to make life better.

What if you take a new direction? What if you say "No more!" How many times have you longed for a partner who could genuinely smile at you? Someone who actually cared about your feelings? Someone who you could disagree with and still be happy?

To have the kind of life you long for, it will be necessary to follow through on your commitments to yourself. The more you take action on what is life giving you, the better and more joyful you'll feel. The following are some guidelines that give you the recipe for success in your endeavors:

CLARITY. Fuzzy desires produce fuzzy results. When you're clear about what you have control over and what you want, change can occur. Remind yourself daily of your purpose, your top priorities, and what your heart longs for.

COMMITMENT. Until you're committed to an action, nothing will happen for you. Commitment means the ability to take action long past the time the mood in which you made this commitment has past.

ATTENTION. Take your attention off the narcissist and focus in on your self-care. Whatever you put your attention on grows stronger in your life. Catch yourself when you're obsessing, worrying, and trying to appease your narcissistic partner. Instead, use the tools mentioned in this book to maintain your integrity.

STAY OPEN. Your greatest good may not come in the exact form that you anticipated. Stay open to outcome rather than fixated on a particular way things are supposed to be. In other words, when you're approaching your life with new perspective using new tools, do so with *no* expectation of what the other's response will be. In this way, you'll learn to protect yourself from further pain and abuse.

When you stop the insanity in your life, you give yourself the opportunity to reach for a better future. I know it's not easy and it may take time, but it starts with the recognition that your partner, coworker, or child is a narcissist and there's not much you can do to help them. Please remember that your life is in your hands; your power and your future are waiting for you to direct them. Only you can stop being victimized and start thriving in your life.

The following is a personal bill of rights that is particularly important if you're in relationship with a narcissist. Please take a moment, read this list, and then take the time to sit and add to the list—or create your own. Keep this list somewhere you can access it easily and remind yourself of these rights daily. This is particularly essential when you need to prepare yourself to enter into conversation with your narcissistic partner:

PERSONAL BILL OF RIGHTS FOR MY RELATIONSHIPS

1. I have a right to be treated with courtesy and respect.
2. I have a right to be the only romantic or sexual interest in my partner's life.
3. I have a right to be informed about our assets, manage my own finances, and choose how I spend my money.
4. I have a right to have a say in decisions that affect myself and my family.
5. I have a right to be wrong and make mistakes without being punished or humiliated.
6. I have the right to live without emotional or physical violence.
7. I have the right to voice my opinion respectfully without retribution.
8. I have the right to have my personal property treated with respect.
9. I have the right to talk to others about matters that affect me.

10. I have the right to choose my own friends.
11. I have the right to enjoy myself.
12. I have the right to live without guns or pornography in my house.
13. My children have the right to be treated with respect and dignity.

(Adapted from Cooper & Cooper, 2008)

How Do You Know When It's Time to Leave?

In our culture, people seem to give up too quickly on their relationships. Ironically, when a narcissist is involved, partners tend to hang on well beyond the time when they should either be getting help or getting out. In fact, many men and women who are married to narcissists hold their original vows as their top commitment. Unfortunately, the pain of living with a narcissistic partner truly tests this commitment. It's a tragic state of affairs when one reaches the point where their commitment is diametrically opposed to their need for safety and sanity.

I wish there was a succinct and simple answer to the question, "When is it time to leave?" It would be a relief to have a formula to reassure us that we're making the right decision. Unfortunately, this is one of the dilemmas that many people face in their lifetime. Whether it be a job or a marriage, no one can adequately tell you with certainty when the right time is for you. However, getting assistance and support from others is crucial. We need to talk about our narcissistic relationships and ask others to witness our stories. The people who care about us can highlight our blind spots and affirm our reality.

One woman, who felt emotionally depleted and abused by her narcissistic spouse, asked me one day if I thought she should stay or leave. As a therapist, it's not particularly helpful for me to tell her what to do; that is, unless she or her children are in physical danger. I can help her by mirroring the relationship back to her in hopes that it will allow her to see the bigger picture:

"You were hospitalized for two life-threatening surgeries and your husband did not show up to visit you or to take you home. You're filled with fear when you hear his car drive up after work, and you've been living this way for the past three years. You have no friends because he's insisted that you don't see them. You've found evidence that he's cheating on you, and you're still not willing to believe it's true—even though you're Fred's fourth wife and he's cheated on all of them."

She looked at me aghast, as if I were speaking about someone else, then broke down and sobbed. She had paid an enormous emotional and physical price by remaining in this relationship. This woman had done all she could in order to avoid her reality. When her truth erupted into her consciousness, neither her denial nor her self-destructive defenses were enough to keep her from the harsh reality.

When that day comes, there really is no turning back. You can't conveniently stuff the truth away again in a drawer like an oversized pillow. These are the moments when we are forced to look at our options: either we will continue to live with our narcissistic partner and accept the fact that he or she is not going to change. Or, we will decide to leave the relationship and hopefully do so as respectfully and in as dignified a manner as we can.

Frankly, it's not my job to judge either option. My intention is to help a client accept the reality of the situation and then help him or her make the very best life plan he or she can make. If one chooses to remain with a narcissist, then practicing self-care, making a safety plan, employing boundaries, getting a life away from the partner, and reconnecting with friends and community will be critical. In addition, the partner of a narcissist must understand that the more she or he does this, the more intense the narcissistic reaction will be.

Of course, the decision about whether to leave or stay becomes much more complicated if children are involved. If a parent decides to remain in relationship with a narcissistic spouse, I would advise her to prioritize the children's welfare and ask her to make a commitment to report any physical or emotional abuse. If she is not willing to do this, I would have to terminate our therapeutic relationship.

We must remember that loyalty to our spouse isn't the only obligation we have. We also have a sacred duty to care for our children and to love ourselves. To nurture our children, we must be whole and functioning. What are we to do when our commitment to our marriage jeopardizes our ability to fulfill our commitment to our children? This is a hideous dilemma that no parent should have to face. However, this question is critical if your spouse is unable to provide nurturing for your children. The difficult question we must ask ourselves is, "Can I really allow my spouse's illness to put our children in jeopardy?"

Although whether to leave or not is a personal decision that takes reflection, courage, and commitment, here are some possible guidelines that may help partners of narcissists with this decision:

- It may be time to leave when you realize that you've given your all to help your spouse and nothing has changed.
- It may be time to leave when your partner refuses to get help.
- It may be time to leave when your spouse perpetually withholds love, attention, and concern and doesn't care about your well-being.

- It may be time to leave if your spouse screams and yells at you and hurls cruel and abusive comments without remorse.
- It may be time to leave if your partner looks at others with sexual interest, states it, and/or follows through with the intent.
- It *is* time to leave if your partner puts his or her hands on you in anger. Since victims of narcissists tend to have a high tolerance for abuse, let me give you some examples of physical abuse: slapping, pushing or shoving, pushing a finger into your chest to make a point, backing you up against a wall or otherwise trapping you, sexual rage, rape, or throwing things at you.
- It *is* time to leave if you perpetually feel physically, mentally, and emotionally sick.
- It *is* time to leave if your partner is emotionally or physically harming your children.

Please understand that even after you leave someone, there will be times you miss him or her, remember the good times, and wonder if you've made a mistake. After all, it's only natural to fear that you may regret your decision down the road. These are normal responses to difficult decisions. But if you know in your heart the relationship isn't good for you, for your health, or for your children's welfare, then it's probably time to go.

When you leave a relationship, you don't leave to be happy, you leave for the opportunity to be happy in the future. And while you probably won't be happy right away, with time, effort, and the support of others, you will be happy someday—most likely happier than you would have been had you stayed in an abusive relationship.

One sure way to sabotage yourself is to second-guess what others are saying and thinking about you. If you're focused on this aspect you will almost certainly feel bad about your choices, or worse. There comes a time when we all have to take hold of our lives and make decisions that are in our own (and our children's) best interests. Those who love and care about you may have an opinion. However, you'll feel like a kite blowing in a storm if you make decisions based on whether or not people are going to still like you. By the way, this can also be an excuse we tell ourselves when we're in tough situations and we're frightened to make tough decisions.

CHANGE AND ACCEPTANCE

*"Acceptance means that you stop
waiting for a happy past."*

If a car is stuck in the mud, most of us will try to get out by spinning the wheels combined with a bit of cursing. The more we rev that motor and try to get out, the deeper in the mud we go. When we finally get completely stuck in the slop, we decide to accept the fact that we're trapped and make a plan of action that probably doesn't include doing the same old thing over and over. This is an example of the transcendent skill called "letting go" that comes from acceptance of what is occurring in the moment. Until that acceptance occurs, nothing much changes.

The first step in dealing with the fallout of a narcissist relationship is acknowledging that we are, indeed, stuck. We've been spinning our wheels trying to fix the narcissist, fix the family, or fix ourselves enough so we'll be loved and cared for—and none of this has worked. This is the turning point. We really see that nothing we've tried so far has brought us the serenity we're looking for and it's time to take a different direction. Or, we continue to rev our motor, strip our wheels bare, and do the same thing with the same results, clinging to the illusion that this time it will be different.

It's human nature to hang on, partly because we resist the unknown. Even though we fully realize that our efforts to change the situation have been less than fruitful, at least the situation is familiar and predictable. Even if you employ many of the suggestions recommended in this book, there's no guarantee what the outcome will be. But even though no one can predict the results, there is a plan for growth and change and it usually looks like this:

An ending . . .
Followed by chaos and confusion that leads to . . .
New beginnings.

Every beginning begins with an ending. We have to let go of the old before we pick up the new. I'm not necessarily referring to letting go of a relationship or leaving your place of employment. I'm referring to letting go of the illusion of potential, the false empowerment that you can change someone, and the strategies that have led you to hopelessness and pain.

When we let go of the old, it places us in an unknown territory that has been referred to as the "space in between." This is the aspect of change that people resist with a vengeance! We were familiar with the illusions and the old way of doing things, but now we feel confused, lost, and unsure of ourselves. We're well aware of what we need to implement, but we're filled with anxiety that it's going to lead to disastrous results. This is the stage where change occurs. It doesn't happen while we're hanging on desperately, it doesn't occur when we've reached the other side, it occurs right in this confusing "in between" state.

Most of us have been led to believe that we can go directly

from point A to point B without spending any time in this confusion, chaos, and discomfort. We have no patience with ourselves, we want our lives to be different, and we want it now. I've even had people ask me, "If I do all this work to be happy, how long is it going to take?" This is where I wish I had a crystal ball and tarot cards. What I do know is that gradually, with support, courage, and faith, if we can remain true to our commitment to ourselves and resist the urge to retreat to our old behaviors, we start to notice changes in the way we feel and how others are treating us. New beginnings don't start with a flourish of music and a round of applause. They start in small increments. Little by little, you notice yourself feeling slightly happier and sleeping a bit better; a glimmer of optimism begins to return. Step by step, your new life begins.

Remember playing on the rings at the playground? The goal is to swing from ring to ring until you've pulled yourself to the other side. You grab the first ring, but in order to reach your goal, you have to let go of that ring in order to grab the next. If we keep hanging on to the first ring we'll probably dangle there until our arms pull out of their socket. There comes a time when we have to let go if we want to move on. The first ring represents our old behaviors and illusions, and the ring in front of us represents our future. If we want our lives to change, we must loosen our tight grip of the past even *before* the future is in our grasp.

When we finally accept our reality, summon our courage, and let go of our illusions, it's as if we're flying through space for a couple milliseconds and we may feel like we're going to fall flat on our face. This is where it takes guidance, reassurance, and faith to trust that well-being and new way of living will be waiting for us if we stay the course. What keeps some of us from letting go of our illusions is the death of dreams that we've never acknowledged or grieved.

GRIEVING THE DEATH OF DREAMS

I once worked with a woman who was married to a brilliant, cruel narcissist. She spent eight years with him and her sole purpose during that time was to mold herself into the kind of woman he wanted. I'm sure you've guessed that her efforts were fruitless and in the process she lost her identity, her dignity, and her confidence. One spring day her husband abruptly announced that he was bored with her and that he'd found someone else who was more his intellectual equal. He packed up his things and his parting words were: "We both know that I didn't marry you for your beauty or your brains."

Naturally she was humiliated and devastated. And even though he treated her despicably, three years later she still feels a sense of grief that has kept her from creating a new life. She can't comprehend why after all this time she occasionally feels a longing for this abusive relationship. She decided to get some help in understanding this.

During our first session she told me of a recent incident when one of her friends wanted to fix her up on a blind date. Although she appreciated the offer, she told her friend that she wasn't quite ready to meet other men. Her friend then turned to her and said, "I get it. You still miss Steve and you're not quite over him, right?" My client was startled and quite upset both by the comment and by her internal reaction. As she related this story she began to cry. "I don't understand this, Rokelle. I really don't miss Steve. I wouldn't want him back, and yet I still find myself grieving."

After several sessions, she finally realized the nature of her grief. Indeed, it was not Steve she was grieving. What she was grieving was the image of the couple that was supposed to grow old together and the special relationship that was supposed to last through time. She was grieving the potential of the family that never happened and the mate who was to love her till death parted them. In short, she was grieving the death of her dreams.

Much of the resistance in accepting reality is that we come face to face with our grief. As a culture we're much more adept at helping people grieve specific losses, like the loss of a house, a job, or even a pet. However, for every tangible loss, there's always a dream attached. The loss of a dream can be the loss of an image you had about yourself, loss of control, loss of meaning, loss of a role you played in someone's life, loss of purpose, or even the loss of a fantasy. The loss of a dream is difficult to articulate, and it's often why grief lingers in ways that we can't comprehend.

When our dreams die, we owe them recognition in their passing. Until we grieve the death of our dreams, we will have difficulty creating a new vision or dream for ourselves. If this rings true, here are some suggestions for grieving the loss of dreams.

Healing the Death of a Dream

- Be honest and name the dream

    Be specific about the dream you've lost. Keeping this dream a secret will only delay your healing.

- Educate your friends

    Let your friends know the nature of your grief. You may want to clarify that you're not necessarily grieving because you miss your narcissistic partner.

- Tell your story

    We all need to metabolize our grief by telling our story and having it witnessed by people we trust. Just because you may get bored with your story, don't assume that others are bored. We can also express our story both verbally and creatively through art or journaling or even music.

- Create safety

   Create a sanctuary for yourself where you can feel at ease. While you're grieving the loss of dreams, be gentle with yourself and be careful of putting yourself in situations that are too stressful or that may trigger your pain.

- Borrow hopefulness

   While we're grieving, it may be difficult to experience optimism or hope for our future. Friends, therapists, relatives, or even coaches are people available who can be the "container" for our optimism. These are people who can oftentimes foresee a better life for you even when you cannot and you can dip into their hopefulness when you need a boost. Our challenge is to reach out to others for this support.

- Keep dreaming

   If you've ever lost a dream that was precious to you, then the phrase "dare to dream" makes sense. To put your heart and soul around another dream may feel daunting. Yet humans are hardwired with the ability and the need to have visions and dreams. Slowly allow yourself to think about, write, or draw a vision for yourself that embodies your deepest longing.

- Gain perspective

   Perspective is our ability to see the whole picture of our existence instead of focusing on the aspects that don't work. If you've been in a personal or professional relationship with a narcissist, your perspective becomes so skewed that joy and gratitude become absent from your life. Through volunteering, getting involved in some service project, and beginning a daily gratitude ritual, you can learn to see the totality of your life rather than only the pain and sorrow.

In any abusive relationship, there are dreams that keep us hanging on to an illusion. There's the vision of "One day he'll realize how awful he's been," or the dream that "She'll finally get help and we'll have a happy family." Perhaps we've lived in these dreams so long that we refused to accept our reality and thus have tolerated unacceptable and abusive behavior. But consider that it's not our dreams that were amiss; it's our insistence that they were attainable despite the overwhelming evidence to the contrary. Keep in mind that with a narcissist, one gets tremendous assistance in keeping these fantasies alive. After all, what feeds a narcissist is instilling in us the belief that if we were just more loving, understanding, beautiful, or intelligent, they wouldn't have to be so offensive.

Before you vow never to let yourself dream, remember that our dreams also generate the hope and optimism that motivate many folks just to get out of bed in the morning! Even though partners of narcissists live in the midst of cruelty and neglect, for many there are children to take care of, bills to pay, and money to be earned. Instead of cursing ourselves for being so foolish, consider that if it weren't for our dreams, we may have collapsed a long time ago.

The dreams we've held about our relationship were precious to us. While it would be wonderful to wish these dreams away, they don't easily disappear. Instead of shaming ourselves, a more effective and compassionate way to let go is to acknowledge both the price we've paid for holding on as well as the gifts we've received. Although identifying a gift might sound strange, please understand that we hold on to our illusions because it gives us something. Your dreams may have provided you with hope during very dark times or even a purpose or direction to your life. Once we've recognized these aspects of our dream, we're ready to do our healing. Dr. Angeles Arrien, a cross-cultural anthropologist, teaches us that in letting go, it's important to create some ceremony that marks an ending of an era and a new beginning.

Over the years, I've assisted many men and women in letting go of their dreams. I ask them to write down their dreams and encourage them to talk about their regrets, the consequences for holding on, and what gift their dream gave them. When they're done, they create a ceremony where they may decide to bury the dream, burn it, or even put the dream in a helium balloon and let it go. As ridiculous as this may sound, the relief that people feel and the emergence of compassion that replaces the shame has always moved me. The worksheet on page 252 gives you a chance to explore these important aspects and begin the process of letting go.

Getting a New Perspective on Our Lives

*"We are so much more than our relationships,
our neurosis, or our problems."*

—Jean Houston, author

Many men and women feel depleted just trying to survive another day with a narcissist. Unfortunately, this demands so much energy and we become so other-directed that we lose our identity and our passion. The exercise on page 253 will assist you in seeing the gestalt of your life's journey, and begin to help you form a vision based on your life's purpose.

It's my suggestion that rather than write, that you draw the answers to the questions posed in the following diagram and then discuss your drawing with someone you trust. Research has taught us that many of the problems we face are not solved by analysis. Obsessing and ruminating about our situation with a narcissist only serve to make us more anxious and fearful. In fact, our despair of not having the answer keeps us from asking

LETTING GO OF A DREAM

It's time for me to let go of the dream(s) of:

The price I've paid for holding on is . . .

_____
_____
_____

The gifts I received are . . .

_____
_____
_____

The lessons I've learned are . . .

_____
_____
_____

I regret that . . .

_____
_____
_____

I want to forgive myself for . . .

_____
_____
_____

When you're done with this worksheet, create some ceremony where you can bury, burn, or release your old dream and make way for the new.

EXERCISE
GETTING A NEW PERSPECTIVE ON OUR LIVES

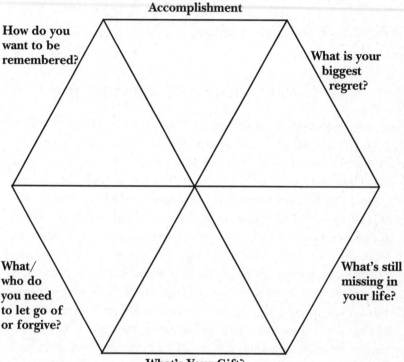

Accomplishment: What do you feel is your greatest accomplishment to date?

Regret: What is your deepest regret or biggest failure?

What's still missing in your life? What is the void in your life right now?

Gift: We are all given gifts that we're meant to develop and then give away. What is your particular talent or gift?

What do you need to let go of/forgive? What stands in the way of your health and well-being? Usually it's something we need to let go of or someone we must forgive.

How do you want to be remembered? What legacy do you want to leave?

the right questions. Even though inspiration and wisdom have no precise location in the brain, research has shown that much more insight is available to us when we can tap both the creative and the analytical. (Hirschfeld and Geiman, 1994; Johns Hopkins Medical Center, 2005)

PERSONAL FREEDOM: AN INSIDE JOB

If you've been in a relationship with a narcissist, it's likely that you're longing for joy, peace, and personal freedom. However, as someone who has worked with many in narcissistic relationships, I know that there's a tendency to blame the partner as the complete cause of one's suffering and limitation. I'm not disavowing that there's a high price to pay in these relationships, but personal freedom is a quality we develop internally. No one can give it to you or take it away.

Inner liberation stems from the ability to face life's challenges without drama, escape, or avoidance. The way to begin this path is by confronting our darkest truths and accepting our reality. Only then can we unshackle ourselves. This doesn't mean we must condone a narcissist's behavior and it doesn't mean that we need to play dead; it means we recognize that these behaviors exist as well as the toll we're paying for this relationship. It also means that we learn to accept our own faults and limitations as well as our gifts and strengths. The acceptance of this truth is the forerunner to our empowerment.

Many reading this book have experienced the alternative: we can dwell on all the reasons why we're too weak, all the factors why nothing will work, all the people we need to blame for our misery, and in the meantime we stay glued to a way of living that chokes the life out of us. This is not to drive another nail into the coffin, it's to underscore that partners of narcissists are dealing with a pervasive and daunting mental disturbance. Of course it's possible that if you feel weak and miserable then perhaps there's some family history or core beliefs that may be impeding you. But be assured, it also means that the narcissistic trance has worked like a charm.

In order to make life-changing decisions, we must listen to our inner wisdom. Wisdom is a combination of intuition, emotion, and common sense. It's not safe to trust only your emotions in situations of such great import. And we can't always make logical decisions in affairs of the heart.

Listening to what some call the quiet, small voice within us often helps to give us our answers. The musician Quincy Jones, when asked how he'd managed to remain in such a tough industry, said, "It's all about trusting my intuition. To me, intuition is paying careful attention to God's whispers." Our inner wisdom speaks to us through instinct, hunches, and the synchronicity of events going on in front of us.

The problem is that if you've been in a relationship with a narcissist for a while, you probably have so many "voices" in your head you don't know which one to listen to. I'm not talking about schizophrenia, I'm talking about the constant barrage of criticism, bad advice, and anxious ruminations that plague many of us. There's a line in the film, *The Gods Must Be Crazy,* when a fellow turns to a stranger and says, "Excuse me, does the noise in my head bother you?" Like this character, the conundrum going on in your head may seem so loud that it does, indeed, seem like others can listen in.

This is where focusing on friends, interests, meditation, regular massages, and other activities will help pull you into the present moment and help you to be the conductor of your internal orchestra.

In a previous chapter, I mentioned that ruminating about your problems won't get you the answer. It's only when we can take the time for reflection, solitude, and creative endeavors that our wisdom can emerge. You may find your answers through prayer, scripture, meditation, or any other way that inspires you. Only you and your highest authority can truly bless your choices.

One day it will become exceedingly clear what the best course of action is for you. This truth will be so unmistakable that a sense of peace will pervade you. The voices in your head that have been driving you mad will give way to a deep and profound knowing. But just like expecting beautiful flowers to grow in a garden filled with pernicious weeds, it's important to clear the way for our wisdom to emerge by employing some of the tools mentioned in this book.

Once we really understand and accept the reality of what narcissistic personality disorder entails, we can alleviate some of our own internal stress and strain. We are no longer bogged down with "what if's" and "I should's" and we can deal with the reality in front of us. (Adamec, 1996)

SPOUSES, PARTNERS, CHILDREN, AND COWORKERS OF NARCISSISTS: A CALL TO ACTION AND COMPASSION

As evolved, strong, or mature as we think we are, no one is immune to ongoing abuse from a partner with an emotional disability like narcissism. (Skerritt, 2006) Those who have been seduced into the narcissistic web of intimidation and control have been under a spell. But unlike the fairy tales of old, there is no one that can rescue you from this curse. We must slowly begin to wake ourselves up from this deep sleep.

You may rue the day when you decided to become involved with a narcissist and surrender your power to him or her. You may continue to beat yourself up for the fool you were to ever trust that this was the man or woman of your dreams. Please remember that the primary vehicle through which human beings evolve is through relationship; for better or worse, crisis is the only way humans learn how to be in relationship without being consumed. The lessons we learn through our relationships are by far the most powerful and profound.

For those who have been involved in some intimate way with a narcissist, coming out of the trance will take some time. Whenever you open your heart to someone, then most everything that person says is going to be important. (Skerritt, 2006) Through the years, the insults and harsh behavior may have become ingrained in your memory. Even if most of what was hurled at you wasn't true, you may still remember it. Your first task is to let your heart break and grieve for the lost years and the lost dreams. By allowing yourself to do this, you will gradually be able to create new experiences and new dreams. It takes time, perseverance, compassion, and patience. As you gradually experience the feelings of freedom, it will become easier to make the healthy changes you need to make.

As you begin to practice self-care, you'll slowly develop the ability to maintain a healthy narcissism. That means that you'll know that it's your birthright to set your limits and protect yourself when needed. It means that you'll be able to look in the mirror and truly see yourself, blemishes and all, and still accept what you see. This takes both tremendous courage and humility.

This book is a guide to help you wake up and come back to life again. It's time to be a hero or heroine in your own life story instead of some name in small print at the end of the credits. Summoning the warrior in you may be necessary to set boundaries, speak your truth, and take appropriate action. But unlike the narcissist in your life, it won't be done with violence, seduction, verbal abuse, aggression, or other forms of control. Instead, it will be done with strength and dignity.

Autumn

'Tis the twilight of the seasons.
The sun is hanging low,
The days are getting shorter,
And the chill winds blow.

An oak leaf turns to russet.
A sumac starts to glow.
The elm tree gives the signal,
And soon all maples know
That it's time to turn the lights on.
In these stately lamps of fall
That lights our way toward evening
While waiting winter's call.

—Raphael J. Weisberg

*A*s this book began with Ovid's tale of Narcissus and Echo, so we shall end with this fable. At the expense of committing hubris. I'd like to give this story a different slant. In doing so, it's my hope that it will inspire others whose lives have been impacted by narcissists to rewrite their own stories.

In this new fable, we find the nymph Echo, raised by a nurturing, strong mother, who by example taught her daughter about self-respect. Echo was no prude. She liked to cavort and play like any other water nymph; but she carried herself with a gentle dignity and a loving heart.

One day the god Zeus tried to exploit Echo by asking her to distract his Queen while he played footsie with some water nymphs. Echo consulted with her mother and a local therapist, and together they devised a strategy. Carefully and discretely, they arranged an intervention that included Queen Hera and as a result, they were able to convince Zeus that he needed treatment for sex and love addiction. Hera the goddess was so grateful to Echo that she granted her the eternal gift of discernment and a one-week, all-expense-paid vacation to another pond of her choosing.

Echo returned from vacation looking more beautiful than ever. And as she was doing her nails in the reeds one day, she spied the most beautiful young man she had ever seen. His hair was as black as ebony, he moved with the confidence and grace of a god, and his eyes and complexion blinded her with longing. She didn't care for the little hat with the feather, but the tights and boots were chic.

With her heart pounding, she pranced out of the thicket and greeted this handsome stranger. He looked up without saying a word and walked right by her. Echo was not a woman to give up easily and so she followed him down the path and tried to get his attention. At one point she stood right in front of him, so dazed by his beauty that she could hardly speak. Finally their eyes met and a thousand fairies rejoiced and sang love songs accompanied by an orchestra of harps and lutes.

The young man Narcissus gazed deeply into the eyes of Echo, and ever so slowly moved his hand toward his heart. (Echo was sure he was going to profess his love for her). However, instead of speaking, he pulled a comb out of his vest pocket and preceded to fix his hair saying, "I haven't seen my reflection in hours and my hair is a fright." He took a step back from Echo and said, "You know, with a little dental work you'd be presentable. I may take your address."

All the other water nymphs who were hiding in the bushes collectively sighed at the thought of being in Narcissus's address book. However, the spell that held Echo was suddenly broken and the gift of discernment shown a dazzling light right through Narcissus. She turned to him and said, "We're gazing into each other's eyes, the fairies are rejoicing, and you're fixing your hair? Thanks, but I'm not interested." With that, she gracefully turned and walked back into the water.

Narcissus, who had never been rejected, experienced a humiliation that was new to him and quite painful. The hurt was so excruciating that it erupted into uncontrollable rage and Narcissus howled to the heavens swearing revenge to all water nymphs. As he drew his sword he caught his reflection in the fountain. "What a dashing fellow you are," he thought and felt immediately soothed by his beautiful image.

Our story ends with Echo, now a successful real estate broker with a husband and two little nymphs of her own. Narcissus, after years of therapy, became a successful model of men's clothing and discovered that he preferred men.

And they all lived happily ever after.

References

Chapter 1: Entitlement, Rage and Contempt

Bernstein, Albert, *Emotional Vampires: Dealing with People Who Drain You*, McGraw-Hill, New York, 2002

DSM-IV, American Psychiatric Association, Washington, DC, 1997

McDonnell, Stephen, Narcissism101.com, 2007

Chapter 2: Narcissism Versus Narcissistic Traits?

Baumeister, R. F. and Vohs, K. D., "Self Regulation and Executive Function of the Self" as part of *Handbook on Self and Identity*, by M. Leary, and J. P. Tangney, Eds., Guilford Press, New York, 2007

Bernstein, Albert, *Emotional Vampires: Dealing with People Who Drain You*, McGraw-Hill, New York, 2002

Hotchkiss, Sandy, *Why Is It Always About You*, Free Press, New York, 2003

Vaknin, Sam, *Malignant Self Love*, Narcissus Publications, www.narcissistic-abuse.com, Macedonia, 2007

Chapter 3: Everyone Is a Little Narcissistic

Allison, Barbara, "Parent-Adolescent Conflict in Early Adolescence," *Journal of Family and Consumer Sciences, Education Issue 2*, Fall/Winter 2000, Vol. 17, 1998

Carducci, Bernardo J., *Shyness: A Bold New Approach*, Harper Paperbacks, New York, 2000

Cline Foster, MD, and Fay, Jim, *Parenting Teens with Love and Logic*, Pinon Press, Bedford, OH, 2006

Crompton, Simon, *All About Me: Loving a Narcissist*, Harper Collins, New York, 2007

Horney, Karen, *Neurosis and Human Growth: the Struggle Toward Self Realization,* W.W. Norton & Co., New York, 1991

Peck, M. Scott, *The Road Less Traveled,* Touchstone, 2003

Solomon, Marion, *Narcissism and Intimacy,* W. W. Norton & Company, New York, 1992

Sroufe, L., Fox, N., Pancake, V., *Development and Psychopathology,* (2000), 12: 265-296, Cambridge University Press, New York, 1993

Chapter 4: The Phenomenon of Healthy Parenting

Clarke, Jean, and Dawson, Connie, *Growing Up Again: Parenting Ourselves, Parenting Our Children,* Hazelden, Center City, MN, 1998

Furstenberg, Frank E., *On Your Own Without a Net: The Transition to Adulthood for Vulnerable Populations,* University of Chicago Press, 2006

Chapter 5: How the Narcissistic Personality Is Formed

Almaas, A. H., *The Point of Existence,* Shambhala Publications, Boston, MA, 2004

Bateson, Gregory, *Mind and Nature: A Necessary Unity,* Hampton Press, Cresskill, NJ, 2002

Bosnormeny-Nagy, Ivan, *Invisible Loyalties,* Routledge, Oxford, UK, 1984

Chodorow, N., & Philipson, I. "Feminism and Motherhood: An American Reading," *Feminist Review,* No. 40, pp 32–51, Spring 1992

Hotchkiss, Sandy, *Why Is It Always About You,* Free Press, New York, 2003

Kohut, H., Narcissism as a Resistance and as a Driving Force in Psychoanalysis *The Search for the Self: Selected Writings of Heinz Kohut* 1950–1978, International Universities Press, New York, 1970

Lerner, Rokelle, *Living in the Comfort Zone: The Gift of Boundaries in Relationships,* HCI, Deerfield Beach, FL, 1995

Mahler, M., *Selected Papers of Margaret S. Mahler,* Aronson, New York, 1979

Marks, Linda, *Narcissism and the Wounded Male Heart,* HeartPower Press, www.healingheartpower.com, 2007

Namka, Lynne, "You Owe Me! Children of Entitlement," Talk, Trust & Feel Therapeutics, www.AngriesOut.com., 1997

Schore, Alan, *Affect Regulation and the Origin of the Self: The Neurobiology of Emotional Development,* Lawrence Erlbaum Publishers, Matawah, NJ, 1994

Shapiro, Francine, *EMDR: The Breakthrough Therapy for Overcoming Anxiety, Stress, and Trauma,* Basic Books, New York, 1998

Smith, L.B., Bonding and Attachment: *When It Goes Right,* www.attachment disordermaryland.com, 2007

Chapter 6: The Care and Feeding of Narcissists

Almaas, A. H., *The Point of Existence,* Shambhala Publications, Boston, MA, 2004

Kernberg, Otto, *Borderline Conditions and Pathological Narcissism* (Master Work Series) Jason Aronson, Lanham, MD, 1975

Vaknin Sam, *Malignant Self Love,* Narcissus Publications www.narcissistic-abuse.com, Macedonia, 2007

Chapter 7: How Do You Recognize a Narcissist?

Akhtar, S. J., "Narcissistic Personality Disorder Descriptive Features and Differential Diagnosis," *Psychiatric Clinics of North America,* 12, 505–530, 1989

Ashmun, Joanna M, "How to recognize a narcissist: Never love anything that can't love you back," www.halcyon.com/jmashmun/npd/howto.html, 2003, 2004

Bursten, Ben, PhD. "Some Narcissistic Personality Types" in Andrew P. Morrison, *Essential Papers on Narcissism,* New York Universities Press, 1986

Cooper, A. M., and Ronningstam, E. "Narcissistic personality disorder" *American Psychiatric Press Review of Psychiatry,* 11, 80—97, 1992

Hotchkiss, Sandy, *Why Is It Always About You,* Free Press, New York, 2003

Pressman, D., and Pressman, R., *The Narcissistic Family, Diagnosis and Treatment,* Lexington Books, Lanham, MD, 1994

Ronningstam, Elsa:, *Identifying and Understanding the Narcissistic Personality,* Jason Aronson, Lanham, MD, 1998

Stevens, Bruce, A Chorus of Voices Conference, Canberra, Australia, 1999

Symington, Neville, *A Pattern of Madness: Philosophical Foundations for a Theory of Madness,* Karnac Books, London, 2002

Vaknin, Sam, *Malignant Self Love*, Narcissus Publications, www.narcissistic
abuse.com, Macedonia, 2007

Chapter 8: Dealing with the Narcissists in the Workplace

Dattner, Ben, *Narcissistic Managers, Narcissism at Work*, Dattner Consulting,
LLC, New York, 2003

Frankel, Lois, *Nice Girls Don't Get the Corner Office*, Warner Books, New York,
2004

Glad, Betty, *The Clinton Riddle: Perspectives on the Forty-Second President*,
University of Arkansas Press, Fayetteville, AR, 2004

Greene, Robert, *The 48 Laws of Power*, Penguin Books, New York, 2000

——— *The Art of Seduction*, Penguin Books, New York, 2003

——— *The 33 Strategies of War*, Penguin Books, New York, 2007

Hotchkiss, Sandy, *Why Is It Always About You*, Free Press, New York, 2003

Maccoby, M., *The Productive Narcissist*, Broadway Books, New York, 2003

Owens, Harrison, *The Spirit of Leadership: Liberating the Leader in Each of Us*,
Berrett-Koehler Publishers, San Francisco, CA, 1999

Vaknin, Sam, *Malignant Self Love*, Narcissus Publications, revised
www.narcissistic-abuse.com, Macedonia, 2007

Chapter 9: Narcissism and Intimacy: A Contradiction in Terms

Mason, P., and Kreger, R., *Stop Walking on Eggshells*, New Harbinger
Publications, Oakland, CA, 1998

Ogden, Thomas, *Projective Identification and Psychotherapeutic Technique*
(Maresfield Library), Karnac Books, London, 1993

Solomon, Marion, *Narcissism and Intimacy*, W. W. Norton & Company, New
York, 1992

Vaknin, Sam, *Malignant Self Love*, Narcissus Publications, www.narcissistic
abuse.com, Macedonia, 2007

Chapter 10: The Narcissistic Woman

Campbell, W. Keith, *When You Love a Man Who Loves Himself*, Sourcebooks,
Naperville, IL, 2005

Fleming, Anne Taylor, "Down with Divas," *Town and Country Magazine,*
   March 2006

Joslin, Phil, Lifeworks seminar, UK, 2008

Marks, Linda, *Narcissism and the Wounded Male Heart,* Heart Power Press,
   www.healingheartpower.com, 2007

Matiatos, Irene, www.drirene.com, 2002

Potter-Efron, Ron, "The Treatment of Guilt and Shame in Alcoholism
   Treatment," *Alcoholism Treatment Quarterly,* Vol. 4, No. 2, 1989

——— *Shame, Guilt, and Alcoholism: Treatment Issues in Clinical Practice,*
   Second Edition, Routledge, New York, 2002

Chapter 11: The Narcissistic Addict: Narcissus in Wonderland

Brissette, Bob in his "King Baby" lecture at Hazelden in 1971

Center for Substance Abuse Treatment. Assessment and Treatment,
   Treatment Improvement Protocol (TIP) Series, No.9 American
   Psychiatric Association and National Institutes of Health, 2005

Forrest, Gary, *Alcoholism, Narcissism and Psychopathology,* Jason Aronson,
   Landham, MD, 1994

Gomberg, E. S. L., "Shame and Guilt Issues Among Women Alcoholics,"
   Alcoholism Treatment Quarterly, Vol. 4, No. 2, 1988

Joslin, Phil, Lifeworks seminar, UK, 2008

Kaufman, Gershon, *Shame the Power of Caring,* Schenkman Books,
   Rochester, VT, 1992

Najavitz, L., and Weiss, R., "Course and Treatment of Patients with Both
   Substance Use and Posttraumatic Stress Disorders," *Journal of Substance
   Abuse Treatment,* Vol. 22, No. 2, 79–85, 2002

Potter-Efron, Ron, *Shame, Guilt, and Alcoholism: Treatment Issues in Clinical
   Practice,* Second Edition, Routledge, New York, 2002

Potter-Efron, Ronald, and Potter-Efron, Patricia, *Letting Go of Shame:
   Understanding How Shame Affects Your Life,* Hazelden, Center City, MN,
   1989

Rolls, Judith A., "The Recovering Female Alcoholic: A Family Affair,"
   Contemporary Family Therapy, Vol. 17, No. 3, 317–329, 1995

Tiebout, H. M., The Tiebout Collection, reprinted from *Quarterly Journal of*

Studies on Alcohol, Vol. 14, 58–68, 1953; http://thejaywalker.com/pages/tiebout/index.html

Ulman, Richard, and Paul, Harry, *The Self Psychology of Addiction and Its Treatment: Narcissus in Wonderland,* Routledge, New York, 2006

Wallach, Michael A., & Wallach, Lise, *Psychology Is Sanction for Selfishness: The Error of Egoism in Theory and Therapy.* W. H. Freeman and Company, New York, 1983

Chapter 12: Narcissism: A Difficult Diagnosis

Akhtar, Salman *Broken Structures: Severe Personality Disorders and Their Treatment,* Jason Aronson, Lanham, MD, 2008

Almaas, A. H., *The Point of Existence,* Shambhala Publications, Boston, MA, 2004

Andrew P. Morrison, *Shame, the Underside of Narcissism,* Analytic Press, London, 1997

Gunderson, J., Ronningstam, E., & Smith, L., "Differentiating Narcissistic and Antisocial Personality Disorders", Guilford Press, New York, 1991, Volume: 15 Issue: 2,

Kernberg, O. F., *Borderline Conditions and Pathological Narcissism,* Jason Aronson, Lanham, MD, 2000

Millon, T., Millon, C., Meager, S., Grossman, S., Ramnath, R., *Personality Disorders in Modern Life,* John Wiley and Sons, Hoboken, NJ, 2004

Morrison, Andrew, *Shame: The Underside of Narcissism,* The Analytic Press, London, 1977

Potter-Efron, Ronald, and Potter-Efron, Patricia, *Letting Go of Shame: Understanding How Shame Affects Your Life,* Hazelden, Center City, MN, 1989

Ronningstam, Elsa, *Identifying and Understanding the Narcissistic Personality,* Oxford Press, New York, 2005

Schore, A., *Affect Regulation and the Origin of the Self: The Neurobiology of Emotional Development,* Lawrence Erlbaum, Mahwah, NJ, 1994

Vaknin Sam, *Malignant Self Love,* Narcissus Publications, revised, www.narcissistic-abuse.com, Macedonia, 2007

Chapter 13: The Narcissist in Therapy

Bader, Ellen, "The Narcissistic Personality: Why Recognizing Hurt and Vulnerability Leads to Greater Self-Acceptance" Practice Development Dispatch Newsletter Collection, July 15, 2004

Jung, Carl, *The Psychology of Transference*, Princeton University Press, NJ, 1969

Kernberg, O. F., *Borderline Conditions and Pathological Narcissism*, Jason Aronson, Lanham, MD, 1975

Lowen, A. *Narcissism: Denial of the True Self*, Touchstone, 2004

National Institutes of Health—National Library of Medicine 2006

Vaknin, Sam, *Malignant Self Love*, Narcissus Publications, revised, www.narcissistic-abuse.com, Macedonia, 2007

Chapter 14: Trapped in a Narcissistic Relationship

Berenson, David, *Addiction, Family Treatment, and Healing Resources: An Interview with David Berenson*, Journal of Addictions and Offender Counseling, Vol.1, No. 2, 54–62, April 1998

Brown, Edith B., *Living Successfully with Screwed Up People*, Revell, Ada, MI, 1999

Jordan, Judith V., "Relational Development: Therapeutic Implications of Empathy and Shame," Stone Center at Wellesley College, Vol. 39, 1989

Karpman, Stephen "Overlapping Egograms", *Transactional Analysis Journal*, Oct 1974

Kaufman, Gershon, *Shame the Power of Caring*, Schenkman Books, Rochester, VT, 1992

Skerritt, Richard, *Tears and Healing*, Dalkeith Press, Kennett Square, PA, 2004

Sternberg, Robert, *The New Psychology of Love*, Yale University Press, New Haven, CT, 2006

Chapter 15: Strategies for Maintaining Sanity with a Narcissist

Bader, E., and Pearson, P., "Overcoming Passivity and Passive-Aggressive Behavior in the Early Stages of Couples Therapy," *Practice Development Dispatch Newsletter Collection*, 12:58, 2008

Carnes, Patrick, *The Betrayal Bond*, HCI, Deerfield Beach, FL, 1997

Giersch, Mark, *Will You Marry Me . . . And Be My Mom,* HCI, Deerfield Beach, FL, 1989

Lerner, Rokelle, *Living in the Comfort Zone,* HCI, Deerfield Beach, FL, 1995

Lieberman, Mathew, "Putting feelings into words: Affect labeling disrupts amygdala activity to affective stimuli," *Psychological Science,* Vol. 18, No. 5 421–428, 2007

Simon, Rich, *The Art Farm and Other Desperate Situations,* Random House Trade Paperbacks, New York, 2007

Smith, Manuel, *When I Say No I Feel Guilty,* Bantam, New York, 1985

Walker, Brian, Lecture at Cottonwood de Tucson, Tucson, Arizona, May 2007

Chapter 16: Building Your Psychological and Spiritual Immune System

Bowen, Murray, *Family Therapy in Clinical Practice,* Jason Aronson, Lanham, MD, 1990

Brown, Nina W., *Loving the Self-Absorbed,* Revell, Ada, MI, 1999

Eisenberger, N. I., & Lieberman, M. D. *Broken Hearts and Broken Bones: The Neurocognitive Overlap Between Social Pain and Physical Pain,* Cambridge University Press, New York, 2005

Grof, Christina, *The Thirst for Wholeness,* Harper Collins, New York, 1994

Hotchkiss, Sandy, *Why Is It Always About You,* Free Press, New York, 2003

Twersky, Abraham, *The Spiritual Self,* Hazelden, Center City, MN, 2000

Chapter 17: Light at the End of the Dark Tunnel

Adamec, Christine, *How to Live with a Mentally Ill Person,* John Wiley & Sons, Hoboken, NJ, 1996

Cooper, Kim and Cooper, Steve, *Back From the Looking Glass,* Tyrrell House, Newcastle, NSW, Australia, 2008

Hirschfeld, L., and Geiman, S., *Mapping the Mind: Domain Specificity in Cognition and Culture,* Press Syndicate, University of Cambridge, 1994

Johns Hopkins Medical Center, 2005

Skerritt, Richard, *Meaning From Madness,* Dalkeith Press, Kennett Square, PA, 2006

Index